RYAN WINTERS

CHANGE YOUR BRAIN

Daily habits for build mental toughness. How to train your mind trough positive thoughts and change mindset for change your life.

No part of this book may be reproduced or transmitted in any form or by any means, electronic or mechanical, including photocopying, recording or by any information storage and retrieval system, without written permission from the author, except for the inclusion of brief quotations in a review.

Limit of Liability and Disclaimer of Warranty: The publisher has used its best efforts in preparing this book, and the information provided herein is provided "as is." This book is designed to provide information and motivation to our readers. It is sold with the understanding that the publisher is not engaged to render any type of psychological, legal, or any other kind of professional advice. The content of each article is the sole expression and opinion of its author, and not necessarily that of the publisher. No warranties or guarantees are expressed or implied by the publisher's choice to include any of the content in this volume. Neither the publisher nor the individual author(s) shall be liable for any physical, psychological, emotional, financial, or commercial damages, including, but not limited to, special, incidental, consequential or other damages. Our views and rights are the same: You are responsible for your own choices, actions, and results.

Copyright © 2020 by Ryan Winters. All rights reserved.

Description

Introduction

Chapter 1 Discover Your Brain

Chapter 2 Understanding the Mind, Subconscious Issues, and Automatic Reponses

Chapter 3 Your unconscious mind

Chapter 4 Neuro-Linguistic Programming

Chapter 5 Begin Changing Your Habits

Chapter 6 Developing Self-Control to Live a Happier Life

Chapter 7 Positive Thoughts

Chapter 8 Mindset

Chapter 9 Breaking Free

Chapter 10 Setting a Routine

Chapter 11 Exercises to apply to daily life

Conclusion

Description

Your success in life is largely dependent on the things that happen in your life and the way you perceive them. While your environment plays a large role in the way behave and think, there is more to it than just your environment. Chances are, if you were subjected to the same conditions as another person, your reactions to things would still be different. This is because regardless of the environment, the nature of humans is dynamic. While you may react negatively to some things, another person may positively react to them.

Considering that the mind is responsible for our thoughts, it is first important to note that the mind does not work independently regardless of whether it is the conscious or the unconscious mind. As explained in the earlier part of this chapter, the conscious mind takes cues from the brain as well as the environment to act. These cues are as a result of our experiences, as well as the influence of our immediate environment. This will help us to gather and process data, make decisions, give responses in a thoughtful manner as well as control our short-term memory. There is also the influence of our biological make-up in the way we think and this is part of what happens in the unconscious mind. The environment and experiences of a person also contribute to this aspect.

While some psychologists believe that nature plays a bigger role in cognitive development, others believe that nurture plays a bigger role in the cognitive development of a person. When one thinks of the mind of a person and the way it works, it seems valid to say that nature and nurture interact to determine the way people think and react to things.

This guide will focus on the following:
- Discover your brain
- Your unconscious mind
- Neuro-linguistic programming
- Begin changing your habits
- Developing self-control to live a happier life
- Positive thoughts
- Mindset
- Breaking free
- Setting a routine
- Exercises to apply to daily life... AND MORE!!!

Introduction

As an individual and as a human, there is a need for you to understand the way the mind works because this knowledge enables you to use the combined strength of both the conscious and the unconscious mind in order to think in a much more healthy, resilient, flexible, and goal-supporting manner.

If you can master the way your mind works, your self-worth will be improved such that you will have much less emotional upheaval and a higher chance of achieving the things that you want in life.

The unconscious mind also helps in the formation and the maintenance of habits, whether good or bad.

Why You Think the Way You Do

Have you ever wondered why some people tend to be more reactive than others? This is regardless of whether they have been through certain harsh conditions or not. Now here is the difference between the role of the environment and the nature of the person. Let's take two people who have lived in a troubled environment for example. Because there have been crises in their immediate environment, they have both experienced a lot of gunshots and deaths amidst other harsh conditions. When they are taken out of this environment, they are expected to become more relaxed.

What then happens if, in their relaxed state, there is the sound of a gunshot? Chances are that while person A may panic and think of taking a flight to avoid imminent danger, person B may not be that reactive because he may have told himself that he has been through worse where he has come from. While their reactions are both born out of their experiences, the outcome of it, which is either fear or boldness, comes from their nature.

This is the reason why siblings who were raised under the same conditions may not necessarily have the same character. While one may be more strong-willed, the other may be more cowardly. Psychologists describe this phenomenon as the role of nature and nurture in the cognitive development of a person.

Chapter 1 Discover Your Brain

How your brain works

Conscious mind: Consciousness means being fully aware of what's been going on around you and responding to it accordingly our conscious mind is practical and analytical. Conscious mind is having an important role in responding to the stimulus. It has no memory on its own and it can hold only one thought at a time. It identifies the information and passes the motor effect to our sense organs our body parts to take actions. Conscious mind is also capable of comparing things. Certain memories stored in our subconscious mind are recorded by our conscious mind to compare the present situation with previous for another one. Moreover, our conscious mind can analyze think and make out conclusions from them. The most important function of a conscious mind that it helps in decision making.

Subconscious mind: Our subconscious mind is in control of all our involuntary actions and is a storehouse of thoughts emotions and feelings. Involuntary actions like heartbeat breathing rate peristalsis movement and function of organs are controlled by your subconscious mind. It also stores all the pieces of information it receives for a longer period then our conscious mind. Things which we do unknowingly are result of functioning of your subconscious brain like free don't feel that we are breathing unless we forcefully take it in our control, similarly we don't it no-no that we start to develop some feelings unless we take control over them with our conscious mind.

Working of cortex: The cerebral cortex is a thin layer covering an outer portion of the cerebrum and covered by meninges. Cerebral cortex is also referred to as Grey matter because the nerves in this area are devoid of insulation that make most of the other part of the brain appear white. The cerebral cortex consists of furrows called sulci and bulges called gyri.

It increases the surface area of the brain and the amount to grey matter is also increased. An increase amount of grey matter, increases the more the pieces of information can be processed. The cerebral cortex has both sensory and motor areas. Thalamus sends sensory signals to the sensory area to process information.

The functions of cerebral cortex are:

1) Determination of Intelligence
2) Determination of personality
3) Conduction of motor functions
4) Planning and Organization
5) Processing sensory pieces of information
6) Processing language
7) Touch sensation

By doing research scientist relate the brain mechanism to behavioral function. A recent article describes how the visual cortex sees. The visual cortex area is made up of 6 main layers of the cell. This layer circuit of cell help to realize the process of learning development attention and 3D vision through a combination of horizontal, top-down and bottom-up interactions. The main aim of this experiment was to show how cortex region helps in learning and development.

Changing your brain

Our brain is ever-changing, dynamic and continuously reshaping itself concerning our environment, surroundings, people and information it perceives, however, our approach or our way to look at different things become static over time.

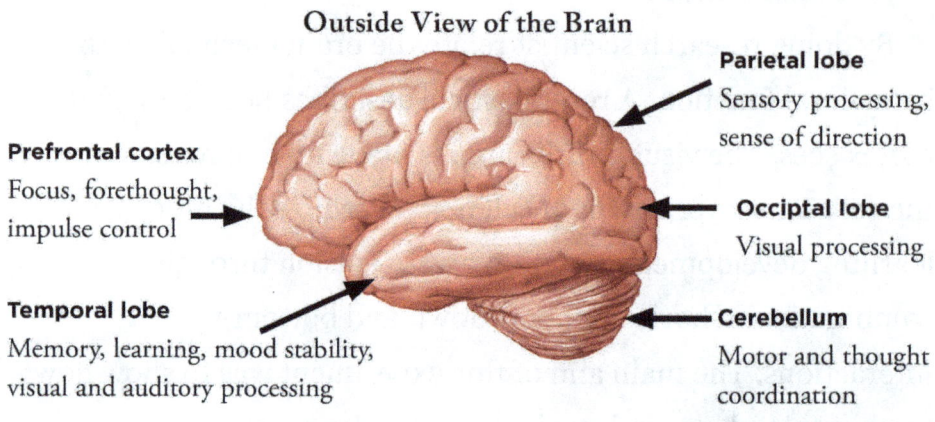

Outside View of the Brain

Prefrontal cortex
Focus, forethought, impulse control

Temporal lobe
Memory, learning, mood stability, visual and auditory processing

Parietal lobe
Sensory processing, sense of direction

Occipital lobe
Visual processing

Cerebellum
Motor and thought coordination

Do you know why?

It all happens because of the paradigms that result from the old beliefs, ideology, religion, and dominant thoughts that we hold in our consciousness. The paradigm is the habitual way of thinking, and influence the way we look at things.

Rewiring your brain means restructuring the paradigm and perception to look at things, situations, and circumstances with a different approach. Most of the people in our time are living with a negative or lack paradigm, they focus on the negative or weaker aspects of every situation. The force behind this negative approach is Fear. But what is Fear?

Fear is simply seeing and expecting something will go wrong in the future. And as we expect, things do go wrong as all thoughts are working for it. By rewiring our brains; We try to approach an optimistic and hopeful way of looking at the things. But what is hope?

Hope is different from fear as its focus on faith that something beautiful is waiting for us in the future. Faith is expecting great things and patiently believing in the unseen. Both fear and hope work on something in the future, but what we choose is depending on our paradigm. The paradigm is not something that can be changed overnight, but for rewiring your brain the best time is now.

Tips for rewiring your brain

We always keep thinking and dwelling about our past and future, as a result, we miss the things happening in our present. The present is the moment where your life is happening, and if we can clear our head, we can understand that it is the present moment that eventually become our past and our future. So, learn to calm your mind, let go of the things that hold you back in your life.

Try to become aware in the present moment because it is the time where all the creation is happening. All the things that we want will come out of this moment.

Rewiring of the brain means simplifying the complex process of decision making, evaluating different choices, rearranging the thought process. Calmness of mind gives greater freedom and joy in life by becoming of our thoughts.

Paradigm gives you a perception of everything around you like people, places, community, and religion. Our surroundings and neighborhood influence the mindset or belief we possess. A habit is something that we do regularly and in a similar manner. It reflects a person's choice and preferences. They are both Good and Bad habits. Good habits help us to enhance our skills, knowledge, and improve our health. Gym, Swimming, reading, and exercising are some of the habits that are considered as good habits as they add to our physical, emotional, and mental well-being. Things that adversely the functioning of our body and hamper our skills and productivity are bad habits. Something bad, unpleasant, harmful, or undesirable are bad habits.

We must understand that time is a non-renewable and limited. To gain something, we must let go of something. We can't have everything at once in life. We have to choose our focus and priorities.

First of all, analyze your habits and then gradually bring up novel habits into your lifestyle.

Engage them one at a time lest you want to lose focus of what is key.

Priority is key when it comes to arranging them.

It will take some time and commitment.

Success is a continuous process.

Studies of the adult brain in recent decades has shown that changing the needs and experiences of an individual changes the way the brain functions. It was seen that the brain functionality halted at 30.

The brain is a complex organ, despite massive achievements in how well we can comprehend and actualize the activity of the brain. Its turnouts that we're still dwarfs in understanding about specific mechanisms.

In times of stress, the brain will take the less subtle path, and use as little energy as possible in decision making, so it'll revert to habits.

Positive emotions are not the only ones that can rewire our brain, negative emotions like stress and anxiety can also have serious impacts.

Training is required constantly to rewire the brain; it will enhance the ability to ignore irrelevant information that can result in hampered brain reaction to emotional events.

Mindful meditation, travelling and staying as far away from stress as possible.

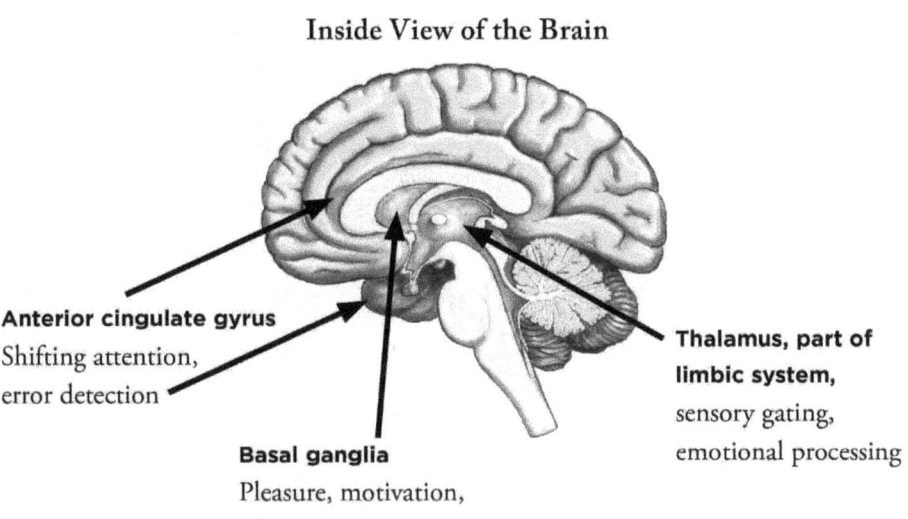

Inside View of the Brain

Anterior cingulate gyrus
Shifting attention, error detection

Basal ganglia
Pleasure, motivation, adjusting movements

Thalamus, part of limbic system,
sensory gating, emotional processing

EFT to address negative emotions and anxiety

EFT stands for Emotional Freedom Technique or Emotional Freedom Tapping. This technique addresses emotions as an adaptive experience caused by the settlement of feeling in the current environment. The main purpose of EFT technique is to release emotional anxieties through the energy pathways. This is a process where anxiety can be released by tapping on specific energy pathway position present on our body.

Chapter 2 Understanding the Mind, Subconscious Issues, and Automatic Reponses

You have feelings inside of your body that correspond to these emotions, and along with the event or experience they create a memory.

In turn, that memory becomes something you think about over and over until eventually it becomes a belief and you start to form actions around it.

From these beliefs come perceptions about yourself and the world around you, and you start living your life according to this memory and chemical construction. In this way, your bodies are directly linked to the original event or experience and the chemical concoction that your body gave you in that given moment.

Oddly this can happen even when you don't remember a thing.

I have plenty of people who come in saying, "I have a feeling. I don't know why I feel this way. I don't remember much of my childhood, so I don't really know where it comes from."

I've had this experience myself. Here is what I know now.

The brain is a storage locker. It saves these events, whether you remember them or not. It harnesses the emotion by the chemical concoction excreted into your system at the time to keep track of what exactly occurred. When something starts happening around you, your brain will begin searching for something inside to relate it to, and it will send you back whatever is found that resembles it with emotional value.

This is equivalent to your subconscious mind. Your subconscious mind is said to be made up of 95% of your daily thought activity. In other words,

only 5% of your daily thought activity comes from the conscious mind, or the things you're actually aware of.

If those events and experiences, with their chemicals and related emotions, are stored in the subconscious mind, in a place that you're not even aware of. If you are living by memories and emotions because of chemicals and hormones kicking up in your system and they are not in alignment with the thing you are trying to do in that moment, you will notice a problem. This is when people will fight, struggle, or even quit a project or dream and say that they are just not good enough to do it.

Here is an example. Your name is a very important piece of who you are. It's how you recognize yourself and how other people recognize you, not only verbally but also visually. Think about it — with the sound of your name not only comes an auditory signal but also a visual one. There are also feelings, emotions, memories, ideas, and beliefs associated with the sound of your name. I have worked with many people at this point, both men and women, who, when we start testing their system, find that they react strongly to the sound of their own name. When your name signals stress in the system, it's the first thing we need to clear. These people usually feel heart palpitations, pain, or that old gut feeling that something awful is about to happen.

The name issue is always one that stems from childhood. The person may have come from a family that used his or her name as a kind of weapon. The stress created in the system was not addressed and, over time, built up into a big problem. You automatically respond to the chemicals created from a childhood issue.

The good news is that if your name is an issue, clearing it is very simple. It's as easy as sitting and thinking about your name, saying it repeatedly in your head while holding your body in a Whole Brain State until the issue releases and your perception changes. I do this constantly as a part of my work, and it's interesting how much can change when that single issue is cleared.

If you think about that for a minute, hearing the sound of your name and having it cause a negative visceral reaction can really screw with your life.

One woman I worked with spent an entire session just on her own name. She was a school secretary and heard her name called all the time. Staff members and students would come into her office, always starting what they were about to say by speaking her name. That sounds reasonable. They always wanted something from her. That sounds reasonable, too; after all, she was the secretary. Because of her position and the constant bombardment of hearing her name, her issues grew progressively worse until she could no longer stand the sound of her name, and she started thinking things like:

"I just want to kill everybody."

"I'm so tired of being in the office."

"I hate my job."

"I hate my life."

"Everything is a mess."

That sounds really bad, but it is what stress does. The more it happened, the more it piled up in her system and the more tense she got. She knew there was a problem; she knew it was getting worse. She just didn't know what was causing it or why she felt this way. Once we started working together, she recognized that in her childhood, there was an incident that contributed to this. It had the same feeling to it that she got whenever her name was called.

Once we worked to get rid of this tension and the resistance to hearing the sound of her name, she reported to me in less than a day and a half that everything was very different. She could now sit in her office and be at peace. I left her with some tools to keep her clear of negative energy for herself and her workspace, and to work with the people who were coming in and out of her office, so that they understood that they were not allowed to bring their negative energy inside. She had to learn how to have a conversation about what was going on, as well as to make sure that her name was clear of any resistance so that when people said it, she could sit calmly and get through whatever was necessary.

Her resistance to her name came from something that had happened when she was much younger. She was surprised to learn in the course of our work that when she said her own name, the pit of her stomach felt like it was rising up into her throat. She told me that it shocked her to realize it made her feel that way — but it was the exact same way it made her feel while in her office all day long. This was a huge clue that there was a problem in her subconscious.

Subconscious stress can affect your life in many ways, and for my client, it meant that simply hearing her own name spoken - made her not want to go in to work. It messed up her ability to get her job done and to do so efficiently.

Getting rid of the stress to the issue meant work was better, she was calm, and was able to get through a day and other issues in her life.

My Past

For me, the subconscious stress of saying "I hate you" and thinking that everything was hard had turned my whole life upside down. From working with my own child who had huge emotional and physical struggles, to working in a household with chores that had to be done and working full-time as a pastry chef where I had to keep moving regardless of what was going on around me, it was always a struggle. The subconscious stress piled up until I had no idea what was going on.

My automatic response was to get quiet and move faster. To try to hide while doing what I needed to. Or to shut down and not do anything at all.

My life was a mess.

Subconscious stress can come from many different places, as does stress in general. Both can come from the environment, your experiences, your repeated thoughts, and even your imagination. However, there is a difference between them.

Stress vs. Subconscious Stress

I meet people every day who exhibit symptoms of stress. The interesting thing is that while they often talk about these symptoms, about half of the time, they don't even realize that they're stressed to begin with. It's quite common for people to be stressed and yet not understand that the body is actually doing a good thing by letting them know.

However, physically, this results in negative issues such as patterns of illness and disease. In homeopathic medicine and many other holistic health practices, stress is recognized as being able to causes imbalances within the body. When stressed, some parts of the body work overtime while others shut down completely.

Here is a list I found on an Ayurvedic practitioner's website of 10 signs that you can look for to recognize subconscious stress:

1. You have become more forgetful than usual.
2. You have irritable bowel syndrome (IBS) or heartburn.
3. You frequently get tension headaches.
4. You develop muscle twitches, especially in the eye area.
5. You have become irritable and your temper flares quickly.
6. You are not sleeping well at night.
7. You seem to be sleeping well but are always exhausted anyway.
8. You have trouble focusing on only one thing at a time.
9. You have high blood pressure.
10. You often get sick as a result of a weak immune system.

If you are exhibiting one or more of these stress signals, it's a good idea to discuss stress and stress management with your doctor or other qualified health professional.

So, how do we know if our stress stems from the subconscious or from everyday stressors? There's no definitive test, but subconscious stress is very often formed in a traumatic childhood — for example, having parents who were angry and stressed themselves, having basic physical or emotional needs not consistently met, or just living in generally bad conditions.

A great many people I talk to say that they had good childhoods, but also have some issues that persist 15 or more years later, with symptoms that didn't make sense. This makes a good case for having an ongoing practice to help take care of issues and stress. It's a good reason to take care of the brain and keep it cleaned out, get rid of old subconscious clutter by constantly doing things that revitalize and renew your mind on a daily basis.

It could be that even that though your childhood was generally fine, there was just one small, impactful event. Maybe you fell from a horse, witnessed a tragedy, or heard angry and unkind words. Maybe you were a part of something that, as a child, you had no words or explanation for that you now have to reckon with as an adult.

I like to describe subconscious stress as something you can't quite put your finger on, or have no real reason for. You may lack a way to properly explain the place you find yourself in or the way you feel in a situation. These things create patterns or cycles that are hurting you and hindering your progress in life.

I know for sure that physical issues stem from subconscious stress when people come to me saying that they have worked and worked on this thing and it doesn't ever seem to go away because they can't get it to release. When there is seemingly no explanation, I can tell that the problem is a subconscious one. Remember, most therapy protocols work from a standpoint of the conscious mind.

Medicine generally works from a standpoint of symptoms. Medicine seeks to cover the issue, not address the original issue. It's like you are trying to convince yourself of something other than what you are really feeling. It's an entirely different matter when you can release issues from the subconscious and feel the difference and see the evidence in your life...

A good example of this is a man that came to me asking, "If I say 'I'm calm and confident' when I am not, the mind has conflict. And that's not good, so what do I do?" This is like using an affirmation. Affirmations are useless, unless said many, many times, and generally only hit on the level of your conscious mind. And while it can make you feel good and positive in that moment, it doesn't stick in the subconscious — you didn't grow new circuitry.

At one point this man took medicine to relieve the discomfort of this issue, over time the issue got worse and had bigger ramifications due to side effects of the prescribed.

The conflict is inside his brain, he lived through something in his young life that gave him the pathways that say he is not calm or confident. It came with an emotional rush and, even now, has a feeling to it.

He took this on as truth and created a belief. The circuits were built, and now it is a core belief. But he wants to be calm and confident. He says he sees other people who appear to be every day. Why can't he?

So, telling yourself something you either do not fundamentally believe or cannot produce evidence of in your life will only lead to conflict. This will persist until something happens that jolts you, or the subconscious is able to release and reset the information.

There are a few ways to do this easily. Meditation will get you there eventually. Hypnosis will get you there if you have a good practitioner. With a good heightened emotional state, it will happen faster.

How Mind Rewire Sessions Work

With most people I work with, we dismantle the limiting belief. This is to tear down the lie, the thing that you believe. It's the belief you have been living by that is simply not true, but that you were told or learned and now act it out in your daily life.

The truth is that you could probably go through your life and point out places when you were calm and confident, but those places were fleeting and you never got a good chemical rush that made it stick. To make the change permanent, we find that chemical rush. You create a feeling that sends a new signal, then we seed in the new information, then bring up that heightened emotion up to set it in place with the feel-good chemicals in the system.

We have to teach the body a new way to feel in place of the old way of feeling that you have done for years. The old way will eventually cause disease and problems in the body. Stress and issues that hinder your progress will keep you in the past instead of creating a great future and enjoying the present.

We must teach the body to find the new feeling and hold onto it and add new circuits that will allow you to continue to think differently. The new circuits are created when you imagine, dream, and decide to live a different reality.

How do I know it works?

The way we know is by experiential evidence. What fruit are you producing? What is happening in your life that shows you that difference? If there is no difference, no fruit, then I know we missed the mark. I have only seen that happen a couple of times.

At some point, you have to start telling the body want you want it to do. You have to command the actions necessary to take charge of your life. Step up and take control! Life is a pleasure and the world become your oyster when you command authority.

Chapter 3 Your unconscious mind

What is your unconscious mind?

Throughout this book I shall use the term unconscious rather than subconscious. The two terms subconscious and unconscious can be used interchangeably.

"Subconscious mind" implies that it is below our conscious ability and less than its equal. As you will see here it is certainly equal to your conscious mind if not superior. The term "Unconscious mind", though shows it is running processes that are out of your conscious awareness. You are not focusing on them from moment to moment. You mind is running the systems to keep you alive, protected and thriving every moment of your life without you even having to think about it.

Self-hypnosis utilizes the power of your unconscious mind to bring about positive changes in your habits, health, outlook, demeanor and beliefs.

Your unconscious mind

Only a very small fraction of your full awareness is in your conscious mind at any one time. You can only hold 7+/-2 bits of information in your consciousness at any one time, that is it varies between 5 and 9 pieces (averages 7) from person to person.

Your unconscious mind stores and organizes

Your unconscious mind stores and organizes all of your memories, experiences and knowledge. Everything you experience in or out of your conscious awareness is filed into your unconscious memory, even if you cannot recall it. It is stored in its own individual way with a logic particular to each individual person. Everyone encodes memory and learning sequentially in a chronological order, otherwise we would not have a sense of time,

but we all have our own individual filters and priorities that make certain memories or learnings come to the forefront of our mind.

Whilst we sleep our unconscious mind arranges all of our experiences from the day into our personal logical order. When we dream, that arranging of experiences (including internal thoughts, fantasies and worries) appears as a nonsensical sequence as your mind creates links and connections between unrelated events in order to comprehend and fit them into its world view.

Your unconscious mind does not process negatives.

Words like "don't" and "never", are not taken into account by your unconscious thought process. If you are saying to yourself "I don't want to eat cake", it is being interpreted as "I want to eat cake" with the emphasis on eat cake. By thinking of not wanting to, you are just bringing to mind the cake; the focus is on the cake. If you were to not think of a purple rhino right now… but it's too late you already thought of it. By me writing that sentence I have drawn it to your attention. For you not to think about it you had to first (albeit extremely fast) think of it to not think of it. This shows you how other people's words and advertising, affects you even if you are not consciously paying attention.

Sphere of perception

We all have a sphere of perception that surrounds us. You can imagine this as a large bubble that reaches to the boundaries of our senses.

Everything in our field of vision from extreme left to right and as far as we can see.

Think of times when you were doing something and out of the corner of your eye you were immediately drawn to a spider or something about to fall out of a cupboard, or times when you were in the street and suddenly you are aware of something happening far down the road, maybe a car crash or people gathering because of some special event like a celebrity appearing in a shop.

Everything in our sphere of audible awareness

This stretches further than our vision. The limits of our vision are defined by the geography of the present location, we can't see through walls and we can't see behind us. But we can hear through some walls and we can hear what is going on behind us. When you think someone has spoken your name you immediately pick up on that and look round, because it is so familiar to us, that we are constantly aware at unconscious level of the particular vowel sound of our name. We can hear something in the distance that we cannot see and immediately feel an emotional reaction to it. The sound of trouble around the corner, the sound of our train pulling in when we are still 100 meters from the station, the ice cream van visiting the street up the road before it gets to our road.

Did you feel that?

Our sphere of tactile awareness stretches further than you might realize. We can sense the heat of the sun on a summer's day. That is an extreme example of course but we can feel vibrations in the ground and also a slight sensitivity to electrical fields. Animals' sense of this is a lot stronger; dogs start barking and horses get upset when a thunder storm is coming and also animals start to flee when an earthquake is imminent. We also used to have this heightened sensitivity to changes in the atmosphere, in a more primeval state when these senses used to be integral to life and death on a daily basis. Over time we have lost this heightened state because it just isn't needed any more. But traces of those states still remain in a very subtle way. Our eyes are alerted and drawn towards movement.

Our hearing is more attuned to certain frequencies such as the frequency of a baby crying, again a primeval survival instinct.

Sometimes you just know when there is a something going to happen. In some cases, this is all your senses picking up the cues at that primeval level outside your conscious awareness and sending you danger signals. In a lot of cases where people who were victims of violence were interviewed after the event, they will say "I had a bad feeling something was going to happen but I didn't trust my instincts." That is your unconscious picking up on all the clues that are outside of conscious awareness, micro gestures too quick to register, incongruity in movement, inflections in the voice and other gestures and signs out of the ordinary.

Smell

Your sense of smell in your sphere of perception, you can pick out the smell of gas immediately because they add the bad smell to it to alert you. When food is rotten you will know long before you attempt put in it your mouth. Smell is the most evocative of memory inducing senses. You only have to smell something you haven't smell since you were a child to reactivate the memories associated with that time and place.

Your sphere of perception is a continuous running sense of awareness of everything that is happening around at all times and it is outside of your conscious thought. Your conscious mind limits itself by altering the size of the sphere dependent upon where you are at any one time. If you are on a lonely beach or walking in a field you will be consciously aware of your surroundings far more than if you are in a busy city. This is because of the 7+/- 2 bits of information. The more information or the busier the location you find yourself in, the more restricted your conscious sphere. You will be overwhelmed if you were to consciously try and take it all in at the same time. If you were to stand in a field with just you and 3 trees then fine, you can be fully aware of the whole field and the trees and the space in between. But if you put another 600 people in that field you will only be consciously aware of those people immediately around you, never mind the trees. Your sphere of conscious awareness is proportionate to the amount of information in the sphere.

Acute awareness system

The acute awareness system is a term I have created to cover one of the main concepts I am going to use throughout this book.

There are times when things are being brought to your conscious awareness, you notice coincidences and keep seeing the same things everywhere. I say to myself I don't see many green cars about and then all of a sudden within 5 minutes of walking down the street I notice a green car and then another one and another one. For the next 2 or 3 weeks I keep spotting green cars everywhere and realize there are more green cars around than I thought there were.

I haven't suddenly called into existence hundreds of new green cars. I am now more attuned to look for green cars and now more aware of them at an unconscious level. Your unconscious mind is actively looking for green cars and brings them to your attention. Your unconscious mind works long after your conscious mind has given up on the idea. Saying to yourself "I don't see many green cars about" has brought the idea of green cars into your unconscious focus. You are now going to notice green cars sticking out every time one drives past. Because you are focusing on that at an unconscious level that is what is going to become prevalent in your life.

Here is an example of how your mind brings to your attention things in your sphere of perception and even creates them for you through your acute awareness:

Phantom phone phenomena; you are going out for the day and place your phone in your pocket or bag, either on vibrate because you do not think you will hear it or on ring tone and just hope that it is distinctive enough to stand out from the background and other ring tones. 10 minutes later you are walking along and feel you phone vibrate in your pocket, check to see if a text has come in or if someone is calling you and find that your phone has not gone off at all; no text, no phone call. You put your phone away and a few minutes later it happens again. You check again, same story: no text, but you can feel it vibrating in your pocket.

Because you are carrying your phone there is an expectation that at any time you are going to receive a text or phone call, You don't want to miss a phone call in case its important and you allow a small part of you to be paying attention to it the entire time you are out. At an unconscious level you are constantly checking and rechecking to see if it is vibrating. But at the same time, you are engaged in other activities; walking, paying attention to traffic and your attention is foremost focused on your visual and auditory aspects of your sphere of perception, looking and listening to your environment. This how pickpockets manage to work effectively, they know people are not paying attention to the kinesthetic (touch and feeling) when there is a lot of visual and auditory information to take in at the same time. (7+/-2 bits of information) You do not get as many pickpockets hanging around fields as you do in busy, populated areas. You are only going to check your phone when it is vibrating as that is the signal it gives to alert you (some people might check when it doesn't vibrate if the call, they are expecting is very important.) Your acute awareness tests you to see if you are going to be alert to your phone vibrating, just to pull your attention to that kinesthetic part of your perception in case you are ignoring it. By creating false alarms, it is saying "don't forget about your phone!" and diverts your conscious attention to your pocket or bag. When you consciously check it, the unconscious says "good they are still paying attention, I will remind them in a few more minutes."

I have noticed that when I have personally experienced this that I would get the false vibration at around the same place on my journey each time. Either that is because when I reach that point it has taken an amount of time long enough for my unconscious to alert me, or at that place the amount of information I am taking in my sphere of perception is enough to distract me from any kinesthetic sensation and miss any phone call I might receive.

Your acute awareness system works through the filter of your beliefs by finding and accumulating evidence to support those beliefs. There will be things that you have a strong belief about because the evidence is constantly being validated or no contrary evidence has ever been provided; gravity, night following day, ice is cold etc...

Then there are things that you have a weak belief in, you are not certain that they are true. You have supporting evidence but contrary evidence has also been provided or the supporting evidence is weak and you could logically reason that it isn't true; ghosts, rumors about people, stories you have been told by a friend about something that happened to them etc...

Then you have things that you do not believe outright. You know that they are made up and that they are fictional or lies because there is no supporting evidence or only contrary evidence exists; fairy stories, films and TV shows, fiction in books etc...

Both the strong belief and don't believe outright categories we do not look for supporting evidence at either a conscious or unconscious level. We do not go out every day with our eye on the sun to see if it isn't going to set this one time. We do not go out every day expecting to see wizards and superheroes. The thing that both these levels of belief have in common is that we accept and reject them without it ever crossing our mind. The strong belief is a fact and we leave it at that, there are never any creeping doubts. The "don't believe outright" we accept as being fantasy and never doubt that they do not exist. They are shut out by our critical factor of thinking. If that critical factor wasn't in place then we would believe everything we read, watch on TV and are told.

But the weak beliefs, they can oscillate between believing them and doubting them in a split second. We find evidence both externally and internally to support those weak beliefs but then that evidence is rejected through to either a contrary piece of supporting evidence or the strength of another existing belief counteracting against the weak belief.

Weak beliefs can be positive, negative or neutral.

1. A positive weak belief is where you only just believe something positive about yourself but then doubts creep in making you unsure. "I should be able to do that"

2. A negative weak belief is where doubt is the main component but then you have moments where you just want to go for it. "I couldn't do that."
3. A neutral weak belief is one that doesn't affect you either way. It has no consequence to you. "I might not be able to hang glide." If you have no intention of every trying it. It is still negative in essence but is far removed from your experience enough not to matter. "If I played for Arsenal, I might probably be good." This is positive in essence but again removed from your experience enough not to affect you day to day life (apologies to all hang gliders and premier league footballers reading this.)

When a belief is weak and we are oscillating between doubt and belief our acute awareness is giving mixed signals, it is both rejecting and accepting evidence in support and contrary to the belief.

One moment our mind is made up and we are certain and the next we are in doubt once more until concrete evidence is found.

Sometimes that concrete evidence is never supplied and the belief remains weak our entire lives. Sometimes concrete evidence is rejected because a stronger opposing belief takes precedence.

Example of Weak Belief

I should have confidence in myself to achieve X or Y.

This belief might be weak because you have run through the scenario in your head and talked yourself into doing the task, but because you have a stronger belief that you cannot do it, which is supported by the evidence that you have never attempted the task before or you have tried something similar and didn't quite achieve what you wanted.

The oscillation between belief and doubt exists in a state of you believing you can do it when you talk yourself into it, but when confronted with the task you stop the positive self-talk and let the doubts creep in. This can cause anxiety where the weak belief is being knocked back further than it was previous to the task; you had talked yourself belief up but when doubt crept in at the last moment, you failed therefore you have supporting evidence to the effect that self-talk doesn't work either and doubt will kick in at the last moment to ruin the task.

Again, using the same belief, but this time the doubt is also a weak belief. You have confidence to complete the task but you have never tried it or anything similar, creating a doubt that is about equal level as the belief. The oscillation between doubt and belief is going to be higher. You might notice this manifest at butterflies in your stomach or mood swings. One moment excited by the prospect, the next daunted by the task.

The emotions of nervousness and excitement are very similar in how we experience them, with the deciding factor being the interpretation that we attach to the feeling. True some things we are decidedly nervous about (Major dental work?) and some things we are decidedly excited about (Holiday) we can feel the difference and symptoms immediately. But those borderline experiences where both weak beliefs and doubts are oscillating continuously, we are not so sure how our emotions and physical responses are reacting.

When you are using words like "should, might, could, maybe" then this usually indicates a weak belief.

- "I should be okay later"
- "I might be right about this"
- "I could succeed here"
- "Maybe I am good enough"

Reading those 4 statements you can see how there is doubt creeping in and how easily that could flip from a weak positive statement to a weak negative one. Not just by making "should" into "shouldn't" and "could" into "couldn't" and "might" into "might not "and "maybe" into "maybe not" but by mixing the weak words up and using them all in the different contexts by substituting one weak positive for another weak negative. This is something to be aware of in your patterns of thinking

- "I might not be okay later"
- "Maybe I am not right about this"
- "I might not succeed here"

47

- "I could not be good enough"

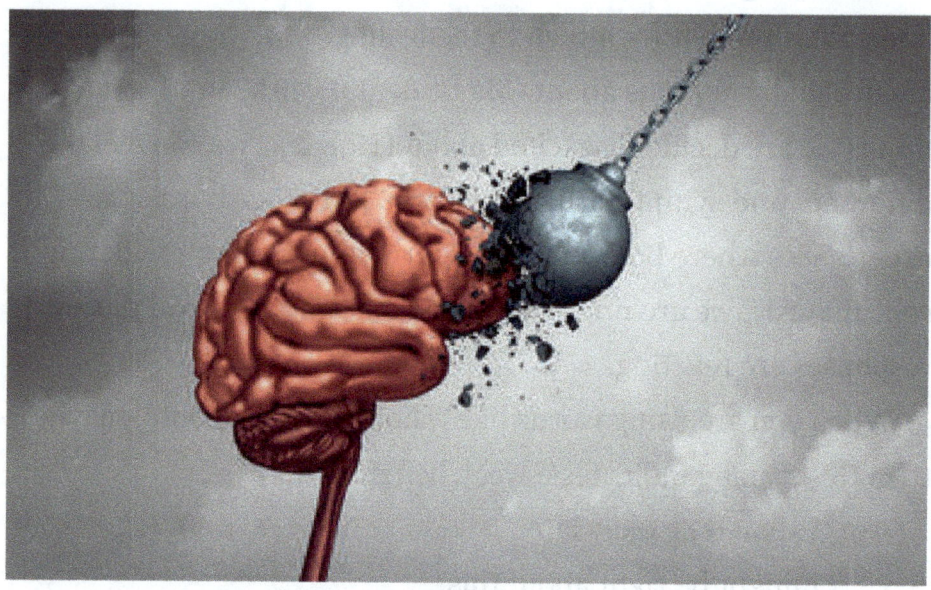

By knowing that those words make a belief weak we can utilize them to weaken negative beliefs we hold about ourselves. Something where previously you flat out thought "I cannot do this." you can weaken just by thinking "I might not be able to do this." Just by adding those weak belief words you have taken a step towards changing the negative belief that was strong and weakening it, taken away some of its power. There is no inner conflict because you are still holding the same belief instead of the polar opposite with no evidence to support it.

Because we know that weak beliefs oscillate between positive and negative versions of the same belief (I can do this... I cannot do this.") Weakening the strong negative belief by adding weak belief words, the strong negative belief is going to flip between weak negative belief and weak positive belief, sometimes you will think positively about the belief (I might be able to do this) and other times negatively (I might not be able do this) which is a much better place than always thinking negatively about it.

Your unconscious is now looking at that situation on a more even playing field and looking for evidence to support both positive and negative versions of the same belief. More importantly it is looking for weak evidence to support the belief and we need to push it to find strong evidence of the positive side of the belief and to focus on looking for more positive evidence and dropping the weak, negative evidence altogether. It is far easier to remove a weak negative belief by strengthening an opposing weak positive belief than to challenge a strong negative belief.

You can do that by placing a belief into your acute awareness system and actively supporting that belief. Your acute awareness system then switches over to automatic and searches for supporting evidence by itself.

Chapter 4 Neuro-Linguistic Programming

What is Neuro-Linguistic Programming (NLP)?

Neuro-Linguistic Programming is a relatively new science that studies the brain and how it reacts and works in certain situations. It was founded first in the seventies and has since been popularized by people such as Tony Robbins, who uses his deep understanding of NLP among other techniques to help people move from a state of suffering to one of freedom.

If we break down each work, we can get a better understanding of what NLP is about.

Neuro stands for the connections in the brain. Our brain has billions of neurons that are each connected to one another in different sequences and paths. Our neuron connections are constantly changing and being updated based on the knowledge and experiences we acquire through our lives. For example, if I were to say the name Bill Clinton, you will likely have an associated neuron linking that name to a picture of what Bill Clinton looks like. You may also have other connections that are linked to his names such as his wife Hilary, his presidency or his marital affair. This shows how our brain works and how each thought can be connected to a whole host of other thoughts and memories.

Linguistic represents language. NLP is focused on learning the language of these brain neurons in order to better understand where people's negative thought processes come from and how to help them actively create new brain connections. The language of the brain is very difficult to understand because our brains are so complex and the language can offer differ from one person to the next. However, there tend to be some core patterns of how we think as humans that can be applied to all people.

How we connect things such as public speaking to feelings of stress and anxiety to how we deal with a break up by feeling hurt and sometimes unworthy of love. Many of these feelings are part of the generic human condition and as such we can identify when they are occurring in others and why they are occurring. The more language patterns we find the more we can help others to break the pattern and recode new and more empowering patterns.

Programming is usually used in the IT world and refers to changing or updating old programs for computer software. However, seeing as NLP looks at the brain from a science perspective, we can view it as something similar to a computer. With certain processes and thoughts creating certain outcomes, we can therefore theoretically recode or program the brain to think different thoughts to create other, more desired outcomes. While NLP can sometimes be more of an art than a science, the programming of people's brains is often up to the person themselves. The role of NLP practitioners is not to act as a savior who will reprogram a person's brain to rid them of any negative or defeating thought patterns, rather it is their job to help empower people to learn and identify these patterns in themselves so that they can transform their own thoughts and thus their life experiences as a result.

NLP Presuppositions

NLP does not assume that everything it teaches is based on core, undeniable truths. It acknowledges the fact that many of its teachings can be subjective and because it is a science that is still evolving and changing it bases itself on many presuppositions. These presuppositions or beliefs of NLP are there to help empower individuals. Whether they are 100 percent true or not is irrelevant if the desired results can be obtained through the belief that they are true. While there are many NLP presuppositions, they can be categorized into six main ones. These are:

The map is not the territory

Taking on this belief tends to lead to a person become much more tolerant of other people and their different points of view. While many people believe that their point of view is correct and that it is the one true belief, this is almost always not true. Everyone experiences life through a different lens, as nobody has the exact same experiences. Even if they did, two people would interpret those experiences differently. Therefore, nobody can definitively say that their view of the world is how it really is. We are all only looking at a specific snapshot of the map and we cannot see the whole territory. We may say some of the main roads and towns but the Mao doesn't show us all the undulations of the hills and the potholes that exist along each road. Realizing that your view of the world is not exactly correct is the first step to opening your mind up to considering other people's opinions. All conflict is as a result of people believing their maps are the territory. Once we ditch this belief it allows us the freedom to grow and learn about other maps and other views of the world.

The past doesn't equal the future

Many people carry a false belief that what happened to them in the past is destined to happen to them again in the future. They believe that they are destined to repeat the same mistakes they have in the past because it's part of who they are. They believe that their character and abilities are fixed. NLP goes against this belief and suggests that our past does not have to be a predictor of our future unless we want it to be. NLP believes that we can put in the effort to work on our past failures or mistakes so that we can prevent them from happening again. It believes in a person's ability to change negative thought patterns and extol limiting beliefs in order to be successful in the future. This belief is at the core of personal growth and an empowered mindset. Many people like to live with the belief that their past will equal their future because it takes the responsibility out of their hands. Realizing you can grow and develop any skill you need, requires you put in the work to get there. It is much easier to play the victim role and blame other people or external circumstances for your situation. For example, someone may say they will never get a good job because they always get too nervous in job interviews. This may be true for now but getting nervous in a job interview is something that many people experience and it is only by working on controlling the nerves that the desired future result can be met. Living with the belief that all job interviews in the future will go badly will ensure that is exactly what happens.

Everything is Achievable

NLP practitioners believe that anything and everything is achievable. Everything in life is simply a problem to be solved. We might not know exactly how to achieve something right now but we know there are certain steps we can take to tackle the problem. Holding this belief allows people to open up their minds to unlimited possibilities for their futures. It helps people realize that there is no limit to their potential for personal growth and that any fears or worries they may be living with can be eradicated and pushed past. They can achieve anything they really put their minds to and they can grow into the amazing person they wish to become.

Empowerment comes from Responsibility

The role of an NLP practitioner is to help empower people to help themselves. While psychologists and some other professions try to solve people's problems for them, NLP practitioners try to get people to challenge their own existing mindsets and take responsibility for changing them. Rewiring your brain is not a quick fix solution. It as a process that you must live by daily and in order to achieve any form of long-term results, you must take responsibility for your mindset into your own hands. In Spiderman, there is a great quote saying, "With great power, comes great responsibility." But in fact, the opposite is also true. With great responsibility, comes great power. By taking full responsibility for everything in your life you have the power to change it. This requires you to turn away from the victim mentality where you believe life happens to you. Empowered people believe life happens for them.

Age is not necessarily a good judge of maturity. We develop maturity as we accept more and more responsibility for our lives. While everything that happens to you in your life may not be your fault, it is still your responsibility to deal with what happens to you. To use an extreme example, you may become paralyzed in a car accident that was the result of a drunk driver crashing into you. You could live the rest of your life wallowing in self-pity and blaming the other driver for your situation and not too many people would blame you. But you can also decide to take responsibility for your new situation and decide that you are going to be happy despite your circumstances. You can decide you are going to figure out a way to walk again. You can find fun activities to do in the meantime to keep your spirits up. You don't have to be the victim of your circumstances.

People respond to perception, not reality

We tend to often judge what happens to us based on our perception of events. We judge other people based on what they say and do yet we judge ourselves based on our intentions. We hold ourselves to a different standard than we do others. For example, presume you were playing baseball with some friends. It's your turn to bat and you swing and miss the first ball. Someone behind you starts laughing. You immediately become angry and spiteful towards this person for laughing at your missed swing. In reality, the person was actually chatting with another friend and laughing at a story he was being told. You never considered this possibility however and you judged his actions based on your own perception of reality. A perception that puts you at the focus. You may often think that everything people say or do is in a reaction towards you in some way. When the roles are reversed however and you are the one laughing just after a person swings, you won't see it as being rude because you were not intentionally laughing at them. You judge yourself by your intentions even when your actions may be rude towards the other person. NLP practitioners are aware that we respond to things based on our limited view of them and often from a directly personal perspective.

Chapter 5 Begin Changing Your Habits

It is time now to begin looking at the issues you have with some of your habits in the face and to replace them with more enriching, and greatly positive ones. Do your best to remain judgment-free while you are doing this, and to forgive yourself for any minor setbacks.

Before you begin trying to change certain habits, it may be best to try to assess what level of change you are at.

This is another point where access to your notebook would be helpful.

The Stages of Change

Look over the list you made of habits you want to instill in your life.

Now, we are going to go through what is called the Stages of Change: The Transtheoretical Model was written in the 1970s by psychologists who were observing people who were trying to quit smoking. They wanted to record the various stages in which they all traveled through that would eventually lead them to take a proactive approach in their healthcare.

The stages are listed as follows:

1. **Precontemplation:** People in this stage don't plan to take action in the foreseeable future, which is defined as within at least six months. People here are usually not aware that their behavior isn't good for them or others. They are not aware of the many pros that exist should they decide to change their behavior.
2. **Contemplation:** People in this stage actually begin intended to start down the healthy path in the foreseeable future, at least the next six months. People may not see that their behavior is problematic, and are more thoughtful about the pros that are involved with their decisions to make a change.
3. **Preparation:** People are ready in this stage to take action within the next 30 days. People begin taking small steps forward, and believe that this change will help them to live a healthier life.
4. **Action:** Within this stage, people have taken action to change their behavior and intend to keep moving forward with this change.
5. **Maintenance:** At this stage, people have been able to sustain their behavior change for at least six months now, and intend to maintain this behavior going forward in their lives. People in this stage also work to prevent relapsing back into old, unhealthy behaviors.
6. **Termination:** Within this final stage, people have no desire to return back to their unhealthy behavior, and are

confident that they are not going to relapse. (This stage is rarely reached as it is very definite; it is usually only used when describing health problems and their changes).

Actual Neural Rewiring

The use of the word 'rewiring' in this book title wasn't written for show. The science of neurology, which is the study of the brain and how it affects human thought and behavior, has proven that there are various ways that humans can actually reshape the flow of neurons moving through their spine and brain. It was once thought that every person's brain is wired a certain way, and very little can be done about it throughout their lives. Thankfully, through the application of new behaviors and experiences, this is not a fact and something you have vast control over.

Neuroplasticity refers to your brain's ability to reorganize, both physically, functionally, throughout your entire life with influences from the environment, your behavior, thinking, and emotions. Neural pruning refers to the natural process of the brain to extinguish any neuron that isn't being fired. You strengthen certain neural pathways the more you engage in the same thought patterns, behavior, emotions, interactions, etc. This is essentially how learning a new skill works; you start off one way, and if you participate in this hobby on a consistent basis, the neural pathway that is associated with it will become stronger, warmer, and more instantly activated.

This process is the key to understanding how instilling new habits work. There is a reason why when you tried to stretch your injured muscles only three times last week, then forgot one week, and then only did it twice another, that this behavior did not become a habit. The neural pathway simply wasn't warm enough, and neurons are only going to fire when they are being summoned often.

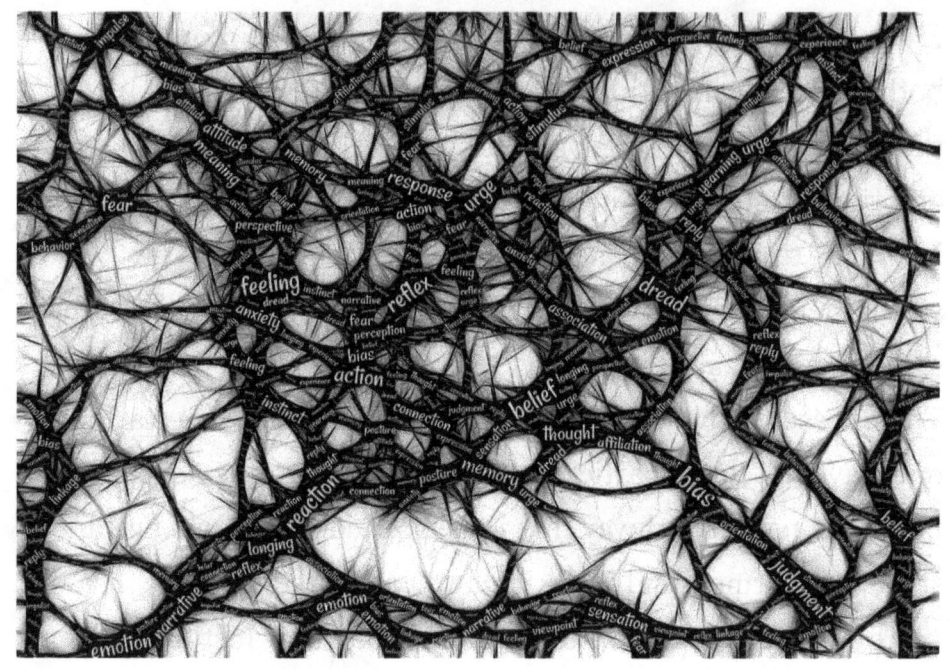

Steps to Take to Begin Creating New Habits

The following is a template that you can apply to any of the habits that you want to create for yourself, along with the ones you want to get rid of. Read this section over a few times before writing it out again in your notebook, for each new habit that you want to form.

1. **Identify Cues:** There is something that has to trigger a habit, and a cue can be really anything that relates to it; maybe stress makes you want food, alcohol, or a certain thought or post on social media makes you want to

procrastinate. Whatever it may be, try to notice these. If this is hard for you to do, try to notice when you are engaging in a bad habit, and then going back from there. Did someone say something to you? Did you read something on the internet? Are you worried about something? Do you best to honestly reflect yourself.

2. **Disrupt:** Once you have noticed the cues that are triggering your chosen bad habit, you can begin trying to throw it off. For example, if reading something on social media makes you feel bad about yourself and your skills, which makes you want to sit on the couch and procrastinate, try limiting your social media activity, or at least not doing it in the morning or the time you feel most affected.

3. **Replace:** Research has shown that if you have a more positive habit in mind to replace a bad one, you are more likely to stop participating in the bad one. The new habit interferes with the old one, making it harder for your brain to go on autopilot and go down the path with those warm neural pathways. A good example of this is trying to replace night-time snacks with fruit or something healthier; not having junk food available may also be another step-in disarming that bad eating habit.

4. **Keep it Simple:** Making new behaviors simply goes in line with the old behaviors; those were easy too, which is why you have engaged in them for so long. Making a new

habit too difficult will make the application of it far less appealing.

5. **Think Long Term:** Habits generally form because they satisfy short-term impulses. The results though of these short-term impulses may last a while though, such as avoiding cleaning the dishes or stretching your injured leg. When you are engaging in new habits, try to think about the long-term effects that this will have on your life, and how you are doing it for the best for yourself.

6. **Persist:** Habits are hard to break; that's why there are so many books written about forming new ones! We order in at night because it is easy, and we don't want to make dinner. This may be because we had a long, tiring day at work, and/or we did not bring enough food for lunch and can't be bothered to rummage up a home-cooked meal. We also may have no brought the right amount of food for lunch because we did not plan ahead the night before, staying up late and lying on the couch. This kind of habit connects to many other bad habits, so, if we look at this as an example, where to begin would be to start making lunches for the week that are substantial enough to feel full of. Then, at the end of the day, you will have more energy to actually cook a healthier, financially sound dinner.

Instilling a new habit is going to take time. While you are looking over your list of new behavioral habits to apply, take a glance at this next list, which will give you advice on how you can improve your mental strength while putting in the effort to make healthier, happier choices.

1. **Create Behavioral Experiments to Challenge Your Self-Limiting Beliefs:** There is probably more than one reason why you haven't been able to keep up with a certain habit in your life. You may suffer from mental health disorders, or even have become used to self-diminishing dialogue. Whatever it may be, it doesn't make you less capable than anyone else or mean that you possess less mental strength than other people. Your self-limiting beliefs are simply trying to convince you of these lies. As previously stated, some of these self-limiting beliefs have the ability to turn into self-fulfilling prophecies, because you are only expecting a negative result, or that no one is going to like you. So, you may need to change those first before you start looking at behavioral habits.

2. **Replace Victim Language with Empowering Statements:** Self-limiting beliefs are more than likely going to be made worse by the constant use of victim language. You may employ this within your self-dialogue on the daily. If you catch yourself blaming others for how

you feel, or the negative circumstances in your life, stop yourself. This is the victim language. It makes you feel like you are not in control of your daily life. Try to replace it with statements that you feel like you ARE in control; because you are! You deserve to recognize that you are in the driver's seat of the life that you are living in.

3. **Practice Self-Compassion:** Calling yourself names and putting yourself down isn't going to motivate you to try again, or to try anything else that is challenging for the matter.

    If you want to do better, think about how you would talk to someone you love after they make a mistake or something negative happens in their lives. If you are a reasonable person, you wouldn't sit and insult them for hours on end. You would show them compassion, empathy, and support them into making new decisions about the future. Try to do this for yourself, and recognize that this is only going to help you in the long run, as bringing yourself down is only going to make you feel unhealthier and unhappy.

4. **Behave like the Person You Want to Become:** Wishing that you could be a certain way isn't going to make it happen. Wishing that you could be a morning person or a person that exercises daily, isn't going to do anything, but

make you feel bad for yourself. You are capable of becoming these things, and the first step toward that becoming is trying to act like that person. Ask yourself, what would a morning person too? And follow through on those answers.

5. **Live in The Moment:** This is going to be a repeated notion throughout this book, as lack of living the moment is a consistent cause of unhappiness, lack of health, and various mental health disorders. Staying within the moment and getting what you can out of it is the only way that you can improve yourself, and reach the future that you have been planning for.

Since there are many habits that people, in general, want to instill in these lives, this book will explore some of the more common and pervasive habits that can help you're as a whole. What will be covered in the rest of this chapter will be the habit of creating boundaries, becoming more assertive, learning how to constructively problem solve, and how to how to stick to certain daily schedules.

Chapter 6 Developing Self-Control to Live a Happier Life

Definition of Self-Control

Your ability to regulate and alter your predominant response is defined as self-control.

Essentially, it is your ability to manage your emotions, your feelings and the action that you take. It is your ability to delay short-term gratification (which is not something that's easy to do, admittedly), and to hold out for the bigger benefit in the long-term.

Essentially, it is the ability to sacrifice your short-term happiness for the promise of even greater happiness in the future. The sacrifice though is something that a lot of people struggle with.

Not everyone is going to be comfortable, or even have the willpower that is strong enough to resist temptation and to be able to go against your own impulses.

Unless you want something bad enough, you're willing to forgo everything else, most of the time we find ourselves succumbing into temptation, only to find out that it doesn't give us the lasting happiness we were hoping to get.

Self-control is not meant to strip you of any joy by forcing you to live a more restrictive and guided life than you would like.

In fact, according to Wilhelm Hoffman in a 2013 study he conducted, it was the people with self-control who exhibited the highest levels of happiness.

They were happier because they could deal with any conflicts that came up as they worked towards achieving their goal, and self-control prevented them from indulging in behaviors which they knew were self-destructive and not beneficial.

It was self-control that held them back from making decisions based purely on impulse, and with the decisions they did make, they were happier about it because they knew it was the right thing to do.

Everyone could benefit from having some self-control instilled into their lives. The benefits you stand to gain from having a healthy dose of self-control include:

- Having that driven motivation that many people lack, which leads them to give in to their temptation to give up when they feel like it.
- Developing a better understanding of why you need to make the sacrifices you have to for the greater good.
- Being disciplined enough not to give up halfway when things get tough, and finishing what you started.
- It stops you from acting impulsively.
- It helps you keep procrastination at bay. Instead of putting off until tomorrow what you can do today, you get it done today. Instead of delaying your attempts to try and learn to master your emotions until "the time is right", self-control

curbs that urge to procrastination and motivates you to begin today.
- You're less likely to give in to your temptations for the sake of instant gratification.
- It gives you the motivation you need to push your boundaries and go the extra mile. Each time you achieve a goal or a milestone through self-discipline, it gives you that boost of confidence, pride, happiness and satisfaction that you have accomplished something meaningful.
- It helps you develop positive lifestyle habits which will greatly benefit you in the long run.
- It teaches you to stay focused, despite the distractions that might try to derail you.
- It helps you get things done.
- It helps you realize you are capable of doing anything that you set your mind to.

Self-control is a behavioral trait that is learned.

It requires the breaking of bad habits and the formation of newer, better ones that improve your overall lifestyle.

Happiness follows when an effort is made to enhance your quality of life, giving you the freedom to make healthier choices instead of emotional mistakes.

You can't accomplish a goal if you aren't someone who's got a healthy dose of self-control instilled in your life.

When you feel like your life is going nowhere, it's impossible to feel happy.

Incorporate more self-control today and your future happiness will thank you for it tomorrow (not literally tomorrow, but one day).

But Why Is It So Hard to Develop?

You know that you need it. You know it's going to help you out.

Yet, developing the self-control and self-discipline you need feels like one of the hardest exercises to do.

If it's good for you, then why does it have to be so hard?

For one simple reason: it takes effort, and anything that requires effort is never going to be easy. If it was easy, we would all be doing it.

No, self-control is not something that is going to come easy to anybody, self-control is something that you constantly have to work hard at, and that is what makes it so difficult to hold onto.

Everyone that you see who has achieved success didn't just have it fall onto their laps.

They achieved it because they were willing to do things and make sacrifices that others were not.

They had to work hard to keep their self-control going, and they are still working hard at it every day. It's an ongoing process, one a one-time effort.

There are no shortcuts, unfortunately.

The Link Between Self-Control and Self-Esteem

Self-control isn't just linked to happiness; it's been linked to increased levels of self-esteem too.

Each time, show the ability to exercise self-control over any aspect of your life, your self-esteem and belief in yourself will be the one that reaps the benefits.

When you see the result of just how much you accomplished because you persisted despite how you were feeling, your self-esteem is given a boost, along with the belief in yourself, which eventually boosts your happiness along with it.

It reinforces in your mind that you are capable of doing this.

Every achievement that you make through self-control is going to boost your happiness and self-esteem just a little bit more, and fuel the desire to keep going, going and going.

This desire will keep fueling you forward until eventually before you know it, you're on a roll and you've become an unstoppable force.

Steps to Building Your Happiness and Self-Control

There is no one, straightforward answer in response to the question "What can I do to be happy?".

That's because we are all different. No two people are going to have the exact same answer.

What constitutes happiness to you might be completely different to someone else.

As such, there is no one direct path to happiness, and there are multiple ways for you to begin the first few steps toward building your happiness and increase your self-control simultaneously:

- **Excuses Must Become a Thing of The Past**

Excuses, excuses. They have never helped you out before, and they never will.

If you want to increase self-control and live happier, then the excuses have got to go. Right now.

If there isn't a concrete reason why you shouldn't start something, then don't look for excuses not to do it.

If there's no good reason why you shouldn't be working hard to control and master your emotions, don't create a reason to do it.

Starting is always the hardest phase of any process, but once you get into the swing of things, it only gets easier from there.

- **Go to Your Happy Place**

Think of something that happened to you which made you feel like that moment was the happiest you have ever felt in your life.

A powerful, significant memory that has stuck with you all this time—a memory so strong that it can bring a smile to your face and a rush of good feelings once more.

Focus on the rush of positive feelings that it gives you. That's going to be your anchor.

Whenever you find yourself struggling, make this anchor your go-to happy place, and let the powerful emotions from this memory infuse you with feelings of optimism and happiness.

- **Keep Expectations Realistic**

Unrealistic expectations will only kill your happiness.

Learning how to master your emotions is something that is going to happen over time because you are essentially cultivating a better version of yourself.

Building anything from scratch is always going to take time, but those who have been patient enough remain optimistic and happy throughout the process because they know that good things always take time.

- **Understand Your Weaknesses**

Weaknesses are another part of being human. Even the strongest person you know personally still has a weakness or two, a battle of their own that they're fighting.

But how these strong people continue to remain happy despite their weaknesses is because they understand what they are and how it affects them.

They don't pretend that their vulnerabilities and shortcomings don't exist, and they don't behave like those weaknesses don't exist.

They take accountability for them, and that gives them the ability to remain happy and maintain the self-control they need to improve.

- **Keeping Track of Your Progress**

When you can see yourself moving forward, that cements in your mind that something is happening.

Progress is taking place, and that thought encourages you to keep going.

Sometimes it's hard to look at how far you've come when you don't keep track of what you've been doing.

Tracking your progress is a visual representation that lets you see that you have indeed made progress and come a long way from where you first started.

Map out your progress, create charts, write it down, whatever works best for you that allows you to track your progress from day one is the boost of motivation that you need.

- **Change Your Routine Every Now and Then**

Shaking up your routine every now and then keeps things interesting and fresh.

Routine and monotony can get mundane after a while, even though you may love what you do.

If you're lucky, you just might stumble across something else that makes you happy too, and having more elements that create happiness is always a welcomed change.

Chapter 7 Positive Thoughts

Positive thinking plays a vital role in managing the stress that can lead to overthinking. This feature can also enhance your wellbeing.

Is your cup half-full or half-empty? The way you answer this question regarding positive thinking might reflect your view in life, your outlook towards yourself, and if you are pessimistic or optimistic. It may even impact your wellbeing.

Without a doubt, some researches reveal that personality characteristics like pessimism and optimism can impact many aspects of our wellbeing and health. Usually, the positive thinking which comes with confidence is an essential part of efficient management of stress and overthinking. And efficient stress management is linked to many health advantages. If you are likely to be negative, don't despair, you can know positive thinking abilities.

Getting to Know More About Self-Talk and Positive Thinking

Positive thinking does not mean that you stay your head in the sand and disregard less pleasant conditions in life. Positive thinking signifies that you approach repulsiveness productively and positively. You imagine the best is going to take place, not the most horrible.

Most often, positive thinking begins with self-talk. This trait refers to the endless flow of silent thoughts which keep in the running in your mind. These instant thoughts can be negative or positive. Some of these thoughts derive from reason and logic. Others might arise from delusion which you develop due to information deficiency.

If the pattern of thinking which run in your mind is mostly negative, your approach in life tends to be pessimistic. When your thoughts are positive, you tend to be an optimist- somebody who practices positive thinking.

Positive Thinking: The Many Health Benefits

Experts keep on exploring the impact of optimism and positive thinking on wellbeing. Benefits of positive thinking to wellbeing might include:

- Improved life span
- Better resistance to a common cold
- A lower level of pain
- Lower rate of sadness/depression
- Better psychological and psychological health
- Better cardiovascular wellbeing and minimized the risk of mortality due to cardiovascular illness
- Better skills in coping during difficulties in life and time of despair

It is not clear why a lot of us who take on in positive thinking experience these perks. One hypothesis is that, if you have a positive approach allows you to deal with stressful condition well. This minimizes the dangerous effects of stress on health and our body in general.

Also, it is believed that optimistic and positive individuals are like to have a healthy lifestyle. Also, they get physical activity, follow a healthy diet, and don't drink alcohol and don't smoke.

Knowing Negative Thinking

Are you not sure if you have negative or positive self-talk? Some common types of off-putting self-talk take account of:

Filtering: You exaggerate the negative factors of a condition and sift out the positive ones. Like for instance, you do well at the office. You finished the proposal before the given timeframe and were commended for doing a thorough and speedy task. That night, you concentrate on your plan to carry out even more projects and overlook the praises you got.

Personalizing: If something terrible happens, you instantly blame yourself. Like for instance, your holiday was canceled, and you think that the cancelation was because your friends don't want to go with you.

Polarizing: You see the thing as either bad or good. There's no middle ground.

Catastrophizing: You instantly expect the word. The fast-food chain gets your meal wrong, and you immediately think that your whole day will be worst.

Concentrating on Positive Thinking

You can know how to turn lousy thinking into a positive one. The procedure is easy, but it does take lots of time and practice. After all, you are making a new habit. Below are the ways to behave and think confidently and positively:

Know Areas that Need to Modification: To become optimistic and take on a positive thinking, you need to know first the aspects of your life, which you usually think unhelpfully about. It doesn't matter if it is daily commute, work, or relationship. You can begin small by concentrating on one part to approach in an optimistic way.

Open to Wittiness: Give yourself consent to laugh or smile, particularly during hard times. Seek wittiness in everyday activities. Laughing can reduce stress and overthinking.

Check Yourself: Every so often during the day, assess what you are thinking. If you notice that your thinking is mostly negative, look for an avenue to put an optimistic spin on these negative thoughts.

Practice Optimistic Self-talk: Begin by following one plain rule. Avoid telling yourself words that you would not say to anybody else.

Be encouraging and gentle with yourself: Once positive thoughts come into your mind, asses it sensibly and react with confirmations of what's good on you. Think of things you are grateful for.

Examples of unenthusiastic self-stalk and how to make it into a positive one:

Negative Self Talk	Positive Thinking
I've never done it before.	It is a chance to learn new things.
It is very much complicated.	I will address it from a different perspective.
I do not have the resources.	Requirement is the mother of discovery.
I am lazy to do this.	I cannot do it due to my busy schedule, but I can re-check some priorities.
There is no way it will work.	I will do my best to make it work.

No one try to talk with me.	I will see if I was able to open the ways of communication.
I am not better on this.	I will try it.

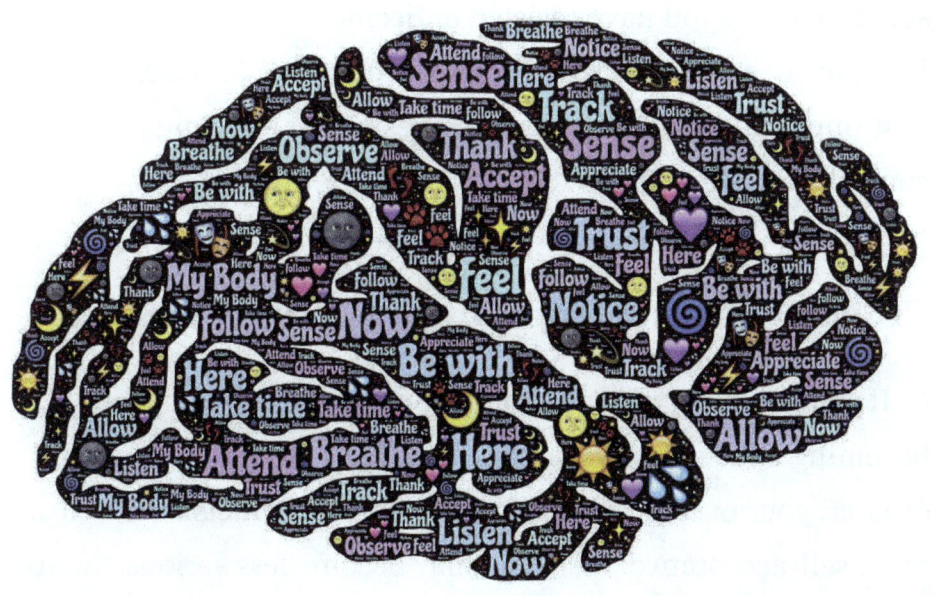

You cannot eliminate unconstructive situations or thoughts. However, you can decide to concentrate on the best things. You can cart off an optimistic from anything which occurs to you, regardless of how small it is. Perhaps you had a bad day, but somebody was friendly enough to open a door for you once you got to work. Therefore, you have not managed to shed weight sometime- but you have resisted enticement and ignored no-go foods in your diet. Positive thinking is choosing to observe the best things and fight the negative ones by not allowing them to control your life.

Practice Positive Thinking on A Daily Basis

If you are likely to have a bad approach, do not anticipate becoming an idealist overnight. However, with practice, sooner or later, your overthinking will have less self-criticism as well as more self-acceptance. Also, you may become less serious about the people around you.

If your emotional state is optimistic in general, you can manage the stress daily in a constructive manner. That capability might add to the extensively observed health advantages of positive thinking.

Overcoming Fear

What scares you the most? Know how to overcome your fears is overwhelming and challenging to most of us.

Luckily, all these fears can be learned. Keep in mind that no human being is born in this world with fears. Therefore, fears can be unlearned through practicing self-control and willpower over and over again until it vanishes.

Fear of poverty, loss of income/money, and loss of failure are just some of the most common fears we experience at this point. These fears often interfere with the hope for our success. These fears can cause us to keep away from the risk of any sort and to decline opportunity once it is presented to us. Also, we are very afraid of a letdown which we are about to paralyze with regards to taking any opportunities at all.

There are also many types of fears which restrict us from being happy. These fears can lead an individual to overthink things. These fears take account of the following:
- Fear the loss of our loved ones
- Fear the loss of our jobs and our financial security
- Fear of ridicule or embarrassment
- Fear of criticism of any form
- Fear of rejection
- Fear the loss of esteem and respect of others
- Fear of losing our partner in life
- Fear of death
- And etc.

These and other kinds of fears restrain us throughout life.

Below are some useful and proven effective techniques to help overcome fears which lead to overthinking everything:

Practice Relaxation Methods

A lot of people who experience cognitive distortions and overthinking find relaxation methods to be useful in stopping the damaging patterns of thinking so much. What is more, relaxation techniques, can also provide lots of physical benefits such as minimizing heart rate, reduce blood pressure, minimize the activity of cortisol in our body, slows down your breathing and many others. There are many kinds of relaxation practices, such as:

Autogenic Relaxation

This technique refers to repeating words to help you relax on the inside. You may think of quiet and peaceful settings and then repeat optimistic affirmations or concentrate on your breathing.

Progressive Muscle Technique

This relaxation technique refers to concentrating on holding, tensing as well as relaxing each group of muscle within our body. You need to begin at your head with muscles in your face and work your way through toe muscle or vice versa, holding and tensing every group of body muscle to 5 to 20 seconds prior to releasing the tension in your muscle to relax.

Visualization

This technique refers to allowing your imagination to create calming and soothing mental pictures, and visualize a peaceful setting or a serene condition.

Mindful Breathing

This technique is also very effective in getting rid of fear and overthinking. This is easy to do, simply put your one hand on your upper body and the other hand on your stomach. While you are lying, standing or sitting (no matter what you find convenient and comfortable), take a slow and deep breath, forcing the air into your stomach rather than just your chest. You must feel your stomach inflate as you inhale. Then hold your breath for a couple of seconds, and then release the air slowly until the last breath is gone. Does this many times as required until you start to feel peaceful and relax?

Explore Your Feelings and Beliefs in Writing

There is no doubt that writing is indeed an extremely reliable and efficient method of processing your thinking and ideas. This is also very reliable in analyzing thinking patterns, as well as looking for avenues to move past those thoughts. There are lots of writing exercises available out there, but the most and helpful one is to take ten minutes to travel around the nature of your pattern of thinking in writings.

Set Your Timer for Ten Minutes.

In which time, write all the things inside your mind, most especially those that trouble you a lot. Explore the conditions, situations, people as well as time spans which you link to those thoughts, and if those thoughts have nothing to do with your personality, your current situation and to those surrounds you.

When the time is up, slowly read all the thoughts that you have been jot down, look for thinking patterns. Then ask yourself, "Have those thinking patterns affect how I see my relationship with others, myself, or the world? If so, know if the effect is negative or positive.

Also, you may find it useful to ask yourself, "Have these patterns of thinking helped me? Or have the number of sleepless nights, and missed chances outnumbered the rare instances I was right?

Follow Your Heart and Mind Do Things Which Make You Smile

A lot of people who overthink everything keep away from going outside. They have fear in interacting with someone as they believe that something might take place. Although you are not capable of breaking out of those thinking pattern, you mustn't allow your overthinking to control your decisions.

If you want to go somewhere like for instance attend a birthday party or go to a concert of your favorite artists, then go. Don't stop yourself from enjoying life. Stop looking for a reason not to attend and force yourself to go. Or else, you're thinking pattern will stop you from doing the things you love, and you will almost surely feel sorry for it. Keep in mind; you cannot turn back the time. Follow your mind and your heart, do the things that can make you feel happy. This will stop you from overthinking.

Tell yourself that the lament you would feel over missing a chance would be powerful than the lament over having less-than-ideal time. Consider the instances you took a risk at doing something new, and it is worthwhile. Think of the instances that staying home or being scared of trying new things has gained you something. You will instantly notice that taking the risk of letdown and disappointment was useful due to the fact that it results in good things.

Always keep in mind that you can leave early when you are not having the best time. What is vital is that you try and know whether or not you can finish up having a meaningful and fun experience.

Chapter 8 Mindset

Our mindset is a very big determining factor in what we make out of our lives. It influences our decision making, and more importantly, on how we react to certain things and how we attain our goals and dreams. People have different mindsets and if you want to become successful in your life, you will need to develop a positive mindset, so that you will be able to reach your dreams.

In whatever you do, whether you are an employee, a business entrepreneur, or an online marketer, you will need to have the proper mindset to attain success. In any kind of field, you will need to have enough faith in yourself. You need to trust yourself that your skills and talents are more than enough to help you attain whatever it is you are trying to reach. This is the very essence of positive thinking; you need to believe that the thing that you are longing for will happen. With this, it will mean that every inch of your body will be aimed to take the necessary actions to make it happen.

One of the hurdles that you need to conquer in attaining success in your life is simply the opposite of positing thinking. Having a negative mindset will discourage your body systems in taking the necessary steps to achieve your goals. The reason behind this is that negative thinking will make you have a lot of hesitations, and the second you give in to that, you will be discouraged in taking actions to achieve your goals, since you may already be thinking that it is not achievable.

A negative mindset would also be the factor behind losing that important motivation that you need to have. Motivation is very important for us to be consistent in whatever we do. Without the proper level of motivation, you will not be able to follow through the steps that you have planned to take in achieving your goals. Aside from that, you may become too relaxed, and will have the tendency to put off the things you can do today for tomorrow. With this kind of attitude, if you are involved in the business industry, then your competitors would be glad to see you relaxing since it will give them the chance to get ahead of you.

To turn away from negative thinking, you need to have faith. Faith, coupled with the right actions, will gear you towards your success. With a positive mindset, you will soon be able to come up with a plan to achieve your goals. This plan would contain the steps that you need to take in achieving it. With that, it is only a matter of time for your dreams to manifest.

Is It Keeping You from Achieving Your Goals?

Do you know anybody who has things they've said they want to do yet they never seem to do them? You know, that friend who wants to go back to school and has been talking about it for fifteen years? The acquaintance who has had the same job for several years and has talked desperately about wanting to find a new job, yet he/she does nothing about it? The business owner who wants to increase sales, but can't take the time to make a plan? The client who knows they need your services, but can't quite seem to make a real commitment? If we're not procrastinators ourselves, we certainly know people who are.

I once heard somebody say, "there is no such thing as procrastination because it's not like you're not doing anything you've just replaced the behavior you need to do with more desirable behavior." According to the Random House Unabridged Dictionary, procrastination means "to postpone or delay needlessly." Certainly, we all have our reasons for procrastination. There are several theories about procrastination; only two will be mentioned here. One theory is that procrastination is a habit - meaning you find something else to do instead of what you need to do; another theory is that procrastination is related to anxiety. Anxiety is often found at the root of procrastination when it comes to achieving our bigger goals; after all, achieving our goals requires change and change, for many people, can be quite a source of anxiety.

So, all of this begs the question of do we get out of our own way to get on the path of goal achievement? People often plan more for a vacation than they do for the rest of their lives! As a coach, I hear every excuse in the book. When it comes to making a goal achievement plan, whether it's business or life, one of the most common phrases I hear is: "I'm too busy to do all the work." If you're too busy to make a plan to achieve your goals, then you're always going to be stuck in your status quo, and quite frankly, you deserve better than that!

Our Recommendation for Overcoming Procrastination:

- Identify your goal - what is it that you are putting off?

- Why are you putting it off? Break it down into smaller events or goals if you can. Think about the rewards and consequences of accomplishing it or not accomplishing it.

- Figure out your obstacles - what is really standing in the way of accomplishing your goal?

- Brainstorm some solutions and pick a few that are most pertinent and reasonable.

- Put the appropriate solutions into action and start seeing those improved results.

Benefits to Overcoming "Procrastination"

- Peace of mind

- Goal Achievement (e.g. Improved Results!)

- A feeling of strength and purpose

Why Are You Not Working on That You Should Be?

What's stopping you from achieving all that you can? Seyfarth Diversified Strategies was found on the belief that every individual has the ability, and can become empowered to be all he/she is capable of becoming. A day, a life, a company, can be changed by understanding and affecting the attitudes, thoughts, and beliefs that drive goals and lead you to success.

Start Achieving Your Goals

It has been said that 60-80% of New Year's resolutions will be broken within the first two weeks. In other words, a lot of people have a hard time making changes in their life they want to make. So, you are not alone. Personally, I am not a huge advocate of New Year's resolutions because I believe in setting and achieving personal goals all year round. That being said, I wanted to share with you the top ten ways to increase the likelihood of success in achieving your goals.

1. Stick To 1 Or 2 Important Goals

Having a laundry list of all the things you would like to change in your life can be overwhelming. Your chances for success are much higher if you stick to 1 or 2 of your most important goals. This allows you to concentrate all your energy and focus on these goals. Once you achieve those goals, you can always set 1 or 2 more.

2. Be Realistic

It's okay to think big and want the best, but it is more important to succeed, so be realistic. Ask yourself whether or not your goals are reasonable and possible. It is probably not realistic to set the goal of never yelling at your kids again. How will you feel about your resolution when your children test you on a very bad day and you yell? Certainly, one can cut back on yelling and work to find alternative ways to deal with misbehavior, but an all or nothing attitude may set you up for failure, and feeling like you've failed can set you up for more failure. Instead, accept and honor your humanness.

3. Be Specific

Be as specific as possible when determining your goals. Articulate how you will measure success and exactly what you are trying to achieve. Setting a goal to lose weight is too general. A better choice would be to set a specific and manageable goal. For example, say, "I will lose 25 pounds by June 30, 2005." Be specific when answering the what, when and how.

4. Connect to Your Motivation for Achieving Your Goal

Why do you want to achieve this goal? Why now? Make sure your motivation comes from your heart, and not from your head. In other words, your goal should be something you really desire, and not something you know you SHOULD do. Truly connect to why this is so important to you. Pay attention to whether or not you are being driven by fear or love. Beware of setting goals based on what someone else in your life thinks you should do. Your resolutions should come from your authentic self.

5. Examine Your Belief in Your Ability to Achieve This Goal

What do you believe about your ability to achieve your goals? If you have tried to reach the same goal many times before without much success, your confidence could be wavering. You could be feeding yourself negative messages without even realizing it. Be conscious of positive thinking. Remind yourself that you are capable of doing anything you set your heart to. Tell yourself every day that you have the ability to take the steps it will take to reach your goal.

6. Create A Detailed Plan to Achieve Your Goal

Let's say your goal is to eliminate the clutter in your home. But how will you start when the clutter is overwhelming? It may be helpful to break large goals into intermediate, manageable steps.

Make a list of each area you need to tackle. Then break each area into even smaller segments that can be tackled easily. For instance, set time aside to clean out old clothes, then to organize sweaters, then to throw out old shoes, and finally arrange to clothe by color or type. Don't forget to specify a time limit for accomplishing each of the smaller steps. Before you know it, the larger goal will have been met.

7. Recognize That You May Encounter Obstacles

Most people give up on their goals because they run into some type of obstacle along the way. Obstacles can be internal or external. Examples of internal obstacles include negative self-talk, limiting beliefs and discipline issues. Some external obstacles are the lack of time, money or resources. Know in advance what hurdles you may have to conquer.

8. Identify A Plan of Action to Overcome Obstacles

If you are trying to give up chocolate (I would never try this!), what are you going to do when you get a craving for chocolate, or when all your friends are chowing down on chocolate cake? Maybe your plan would be to carry a sweet substitute with you at all times. Or perhaps you could involve yourself in a fun activity when the urge strikes. If your obstacles are tougher and you need more support, consider hiring a life coach to help you work through your blocks.

9. Enlist the Support of An Accountability Partner

As you work towards your goals, it can be very helpful to have someone in your life to be your support partner. Consider asking your partner or friend to help you stick to the goals you have set. Use this person when you are struggling and set up a plan to check in regularly with him/her. As a coach, I have the privilege of trading coaching services with my peers. My coach helps me achieve my goals, overcome any obstacles, and celebrate my success.

10. Celebrate Success Along the Way

One of the most important things you can do for yourself is to celebrate your small successes as you work towards your larger goals. Don't wait until the end to reward yourself. You deserve to be recognized for your efforts and your commitment, especially when your goals take a long time to achieve. If you don't celebrate on your journey, you will lose your motivation. So, celebrate, celebrate, and celebrate!

Achieving your goals can be tough work sometimes, but it is also very rewarding. If you fall off your path, remember you can always get back on. It's okay to take a few detours. It's also okay to take a break to rest.

Don't beat yourself up or give up hope. Start again where you fell down and before you know it, you will be a pro at accomplishing your goals.

Chapter 9 Breaking Free

Changing your mindset is like adopting a new routine and habit, but it isn't as hard as it sounds. Once you get the hang of it, you will never have to worry about having control over how you act and think, it will become like a second language to you.

The very first step to fulfilling your goals and desires is to be able to control what happens inside your head, in other words, changing the way you view yourself and the world around you. Many people grow up thinking that if you fail once then you should give up, however, what they don't know is that failure is the key to success. Failure is something that is stopping you from moving towards your destined path, it's a hard test that you must overcome in order to prove that you are worthy of receiving that car you've always wanted or become the manager of the company you've been chasing for years. Nothing will ever be handed to you on a silver platter. You must realize that everything is being watched by the universe, your every movement determines your fate and your every good deed provides you with a reward, a step towards your goals.

Imagine what would happen if everything was easy, achieving success is just right behind your bedroom door and all you have to do is open it. There would be no lessons to be learned, no chance of improvement and no change in yourself. This won't make you the best self that you can be and it sure won't feel satisfying finally being able to hold what you've always wanted if it was just handed to you for no apparent reason. Of course, to some it sounds wonderful, no effort but goals achieved. Unfortunately, this is not how life works. Life likes to reward you for the things that you do and even if it seems like your entire world is falling apart, remember that this is just another test that you must pass in order to live the life of happiness and success that you've always wanted.

The first step to changing your mindset is to stop all the negative self-talk that you say to yourself every single day. All the negative things you say to yourself and others matter. The feeling of anxiety and depression all start with one negative thought and had evolved into a whole cloud of bad energies that prevent you from being happy and living your best life. It is important to remember that you are allowed to be a self-critique, it often helps to better yourself in many different ways however you must be in control of your emotions and thoughts, not criticizing yourself to the point where you hurt your own feelings. Everyone knows it's hard, to be in control of something so big as your mind but imagine the things you could do if you were able to clear away your clouded vision and your self-doubts to be able to give yourself a second chance. Here are a few things that are guaranteed to help you overcome negative thoughts.

Surround Yourself with Positive People

The first step to stop the toxic thoughts that cloud your vision is to stop others from discouraging you first. If you keep on hearing people telling you that 'you can't do it' over and over again, eventually you will start to believe them. We often are attracted to negative people, maybe because they are more fun to be around or you get something out of it. But you must remember that these people love to manipulate you, guilt-tripping you to get what they want and make you feel as if you are not even there. This makes you wonder if you are the problem when in reality that person is. You are not attracting the people in general, but the energy that they surround themselves with.

You might be asking yourself, why am I a magnet for bad friends or mean people? This is because of low frequencies, who are people who are unhappy, who have negative self-talk or don't show enough love for themselves and others. Low-frequency people tend to attract other low-frequency people. In order to change that, you must raise your frequency first by taking care of yourself, avoiding bad situations and spreading love to people around you. You must tune in with your inner self and be the best version of yourself that you can be and the first thing you should do is cut all ties with people who make you feel bad. Surrounding yourself with positive people is the gift that life brings us. Not only do they support you no matter what you choose in your life but they also provide good advice. So when you realize that you are being horrible and judgmental to yourself, imagine what would that friend say in this situation. How would they react and what advice would they give you? Imagine them saying to you, repeat it for yourself a couple of times. What you keep on saying, become your reality. You have people that have your back no matter what, they care about you and you should show that same affection to yourself too.

Write Your Thoughts Down

When you visually begin to see things only then you realize how silly they all sound. Writing down what scares you and what gives you stress is an important part to learn how to get over it. Almost like getting over a fear of heights by going to the highest building or flying on an airplane and looking down. It helps you to be able to understand where those feelings are coming from more deeply than just know what the situation is all about. You finally begin to accept the fact that this situation gives you a lot of stress, which makes you feel that you are not worth it. But after you write down the negative feeling, you must write down a positive one. If you are insecure about your body, write down how that makes you feel and then look back to how much you've grown, if it's physically or mentally. Or if you are stressed out, imagine how relaxed and relieved you would feel if the situation was over. You must welcome the negative feeling with open arms, realize that you are stressed but know that you can do it, 'this situation gives me stress, but when it's over I can finally enjoy my free time'. Try to make a positive feeling overcome the negative. This will help you gain control over your emotions and will teach you to trust your inner self.

Catch That Thought

There are so many thoughts constantly flying around in our heads, which is why when your negative self-talk unravels, you must seize it. The best way to understand why you are thinking negatively is to realize what is causing it. You have to uncover the root of the problem. You often hear yourself saying things like 'I can't do this' and when this happens you must become conscious of the fact that you are saying it to yourself. Interrogate your thought, ask yourself 'why can't I do this' or 'what is stopping me from doing this'. Have a conversation with yourself, figure out the root of this problem then solve it.

For example, imagine yourself rehearsing for an audition, a huge opportunity has come towards you to finally be able to achieve your great dream of becoming a famous singer. You are scared and nervous, which are natural feelings to feel during such situations but then you begin to tell yourself that 'you will never pass the audition'. The first step you should do is clear all your other thoughts and worries, let them go and focus on this one thing. Why do you feel like you can't do this? Is it because you feel unprepared? If so, then why is that? Didn't you practice day and night? Do you think you are not good enough? Why should you feel that way if you put in so much effort? Reasoning with yourself will help you understand that you shouldn't be feeling the way that you are and it also helps you to turn the situation around, to turn the negative emotions into the positive ones. It is often hard to stop yourself from thinking badly, which is why you must reason with yourself and know that your negative thoughts are natural even though they affect you badly, they are only here to discourage you and push you to prove them wrong.

Positive Morning Routine

Ever had a bad morning that made you feel grumpy and upset which then ruined your entire day? The key to fix that is to start off your day right by making sure it goes well with a positive morning routine. To change the negativity that only you hold accountable for, you must first change the cause of it and try to prevent it. Do things in the morning that makes you feel good about yourself and the world around you. Take a refreshing morning shower, go out for breakfast or go to the gym. If you start off your morning right with a good mood, it is scientifically proven that the rest of your day will be good too. But if your day starts off poorly, maybe you missed your bus or overslept, you must keep in mind that things happen for a reason and that this is not an excuse to be grumpy and unhappy for the rest of the day because you will attract other negative things. If you tell yourself that 'today is not a good day' then it won't get better at all. Clear your head and start over, don't focus on the past but look more closely into your future, learn to be able to decide your own fate and destiny. If you want to have a great day, just tell yourself that you will. A good way to shape your day yourself is to wake up and repeat to yourself out loud a few times saying 'today three good things will happen to me' and all you got to do is wait and watch. Starting your day right with a good attitude and a positive mindset is guaranteed to make your day go by smoothly. After all, you have the power to change it and no one else.

The second way to change your mindset is to recite positive affirmations. That way you are able to turn the bad into the good. Repeating in your head or writing down your qualities can help you focus more on them rather than the ones you lack. Feel good about yourself and the things in your life instead of always focusing on the things you wish to have. Although it's good to dream and hope for the better, it can often turn into an obsession which is something you must avoid. So, take a moment right now, go to a voice recording app and record yourself saying something positive and encouraging like 'you are an amazing, strong person, you are going to achieve success in life and don't let anyone bring you down so have an amazing day'. It's easy and simple, listen back to it, whenever you feel down or unmotivated. Sometimes all you need is to hear yourself saying it in order to believe it.

Patience is the key to success. Nothing happens overnight and changing the way your mind thinks and works is like stopping a bad habit because your brain has been working ever since you were born, making its own habits and building the way you are today. It is impossible to reprogram it in one day. You must remain calm and know that nothing is going to work straight away but you will see improvement. Day by day you will realize that you are becoming less harsh on yourself and growing as a person. Every day you become a step closer and every day you must be aware that you are the one who is making decisions, not your mind and feelings. When something doesn't go as planned, we immediately lose our mental focus and straightaway jump to conclusions which then gives us stress. You need to learn to wait for things to come naturally your way, if you try to speed up the process then you will just make things worse. When the time is right, you will receive what you've been waiting for rather than rushing it towards you. The universe sees that when people become too eager and hungry for their desires, it slows down the outcome. In order to achieve what you've been waiting for, you must turn your attention elsewhere, focus on something else and you'll be surprised how fast the universe will work in your favor.

In order to keep your mind clear for your dreams and desires, you must set your goals straight. Keep a journal on your phone or a physical one, where you write down how your day went by, what you did and how you felt about it. This will help you reflect on your actions, if what you did justify the situation or not. Doing this will turn you into a better person. You should write down your goals for the day, month or year to keep in mind. Look back at them from time to time and remind yourself what you are here for and that you are doing this for yourself and no one else. You can also print out pictures of the things you want, whether if it's your dream car or a house. This will work as a boost in motivation and will push you to achieve your goals. You will be able to look back at how much you have accomplished over time and know that nothing is impossible as long as you set your mind on it.

Focus on things that matter to you, don't always hold grudges against people who wronged you or giving all your attention to one single thing. Sometimes too much energy can become overwhelming, therefore make sure to give out equal focus to all aspects in your life. Don't overwork yourself no matter how much you think it will help you. You must find balance in your life, between work and personal relationships otherwise it will start to affect you poorly and others around you. You have to reward yourself and give yourself breaks that you deserve, sometimes all you need is a few days off to refresh your mind and inspire yourself. Rushing things and working all the time can often lead to poor quality work.

Another key point is to act as if you already have that certain mindset that you are going for. For example, if it's something to do with your body, you'd act as if you are fit, healthy and confident in yourself. Enjoy your life and things that you already have as well as acting like you already achieved those certain goals. Of course, you also need to put in a little effort into it, like start eating healthy or going for a fifteen-minute jog in the morning. Once you start doing it and acting it, you will begin to feel like it. You play pretend until it actually becomes real, almost like 'fake it until you make it'.

When you feel as if you are in the deepest darkest place in life right now and you don't have the strength to reach out for help or stand up, know that you are capable of doing it yourself. You don't need medication to get rid of depression, but all you need is the power of your own mind. You have to realize that you shouldn't be wasting your time being sad and unable to carry on, look back to the things that make you happy in life or change your schedule around. If nothing interests you and your life are boring, then make it more fun. There are countless possibilities in the world and so many things to learn and explore, you shouldn't be giving up if you are feeling down at this point of your life, but bear with it, find ways to make it better. Pull yourself together and tell yourself that this isn't who you are, your emotions, however dark they may be, shouldn't define the way you live. Don't cry about things that you don't have or the things that you are suffering from, it's not good giving it more attention to the issue at hand, making it less likely to get better. You're only influenced psychologically, it's all in your head! You make yourself feel the way you do and nothing else. It's hard sometimes, to let go of something that became a part of your daily life and a part of you, but it's for the best in order to get better and move on.

But sometimes you can't control the way you act or feel, like for example having anxiety. It's a strong emotion that affects almost one in five people. Look around you, in a bus that you travel from work or in a meeting that you attend every day, there are so many people that you see every single day, so many different faces that may or may not have similar problems to you. Everyone is dealing with something, know that you are not alone. Accept your feelings and emotions and the way that it makes you feel and learn to turn them into something greater.

Turn your anxiety into overwhelming excitement, change the situation around and turn it into a positive outcome. Reach out to people for help and comfort but remember that the best comfort is you to yourself. Sit down and drink some warm tea or coffee, change the way you view your situation and realize that you are not going to be like this forever. If a mental issue is what blocks you from achieving the right mindset then find a way around it, don't let anything bring you down. Your mind is far more powerful than what other people lead you to believe, you have what it takes to change your own life.

Accept the way you are, don't always be eager to change into what you want to become. Be kind to yourself, you are only going to get one chance at life so make it count. Don't spend time grieving over your losses because that won't get you anywhere. Only when you will be able to find peace with yourself then life will surely turn itself upside down for the better. You have to find happiness and acceptance in the present rather than jumping into the future. Remember to breathe the air around you, clear your head and open your eyes. Don't be scared to face the present and learn to accept yourself for who you are. Stop complaining about every single inconvenience that occurs in your life, be aware that it is only paying you a simple hello before it will leave once again. Open your heart to love and give it to yourself and others around you. Different energies that people carry are like magnets, they attract or repel each other, if you are spreading love and peace around you then other people will be attracted to you. Quality of our life depends on the quality of our thinking.

Stay healthy and don't be harsh on yourself because your mind also needs a break just like your physical body. Get enough hours of sleep, it is recommended that you get from 7 to 10 hours of sleep a day, plan your schedule right because even when you are sleeping, your mind is still working and reflecting on everything you did during the day.

It looks back on your memories and makes sure that you remember them. It clears out the toxins that occurred during the day and refreshes itself for the new day ahead. The most important activity the brain does is the dream! Dreams are important, some of them make you feel amazing and hopeful for the future. They even motivate you to become successful in life because when you dream, your emotions and reactions are real even though everything happens in your head. You can finally feel the excitement of getting that car you've always wanted which will push you to actually get it in real life. It's a great way for motivation and gives you a break from reality. There are also so many medical studies that prove that having a lack of sleep can lead to countless health issues. So, change your plans for today and get a good amount of sleep!

Make a habit of eating enough vegetables and fruits to maintain a healthy and balanced lifestyle. Walking is the most basic and easiest form of exercise, instead of driving yourself places, walking 10,000 steps a day can change your way of living. You are helping your body to maintain healthily and eliminating the risk of having a health problem in the future. Start looking after yourself because a lot of health problems are permanent and can affect you poorly. But also know when to reward yourself for the good things that you are doing for your body.

This is a lot to process, so let's summarize it quickly. The first step is to control what happens in your head, don't get discouraged too easily. The downhills in your life are just part of the tests that will help you in the future. Stop the negative self-talk by changing the way you think. Some key points on controlling negative thoughts are surrounding yourself with positive people, writing your thoughts down, interrogating them, and changing their cause. Your mind believes whatever you tell it, so continue with positive affirmations. Focus on yourself and give yourself the love and attention that you need. Set your goals straight, know that nothing is going to accomplish itself overnight so have patience. Know that you have the power to change but first accept yourself for who you are, you can't change yourself to be a completely different person but you can upgrade yourself to be the best version of yourself that you can be. Fake it until you make it, act as if you own it and have it, all you got to do is figure out how to obtain it.

The universe already knows the answer to that question, and it will start dropping hints sooner or later. Finally, get plenty of sleep and stay healthy. Help your body to get rid of toxins by eating healthy, it will thank you later in the future. Success is just around the corner.

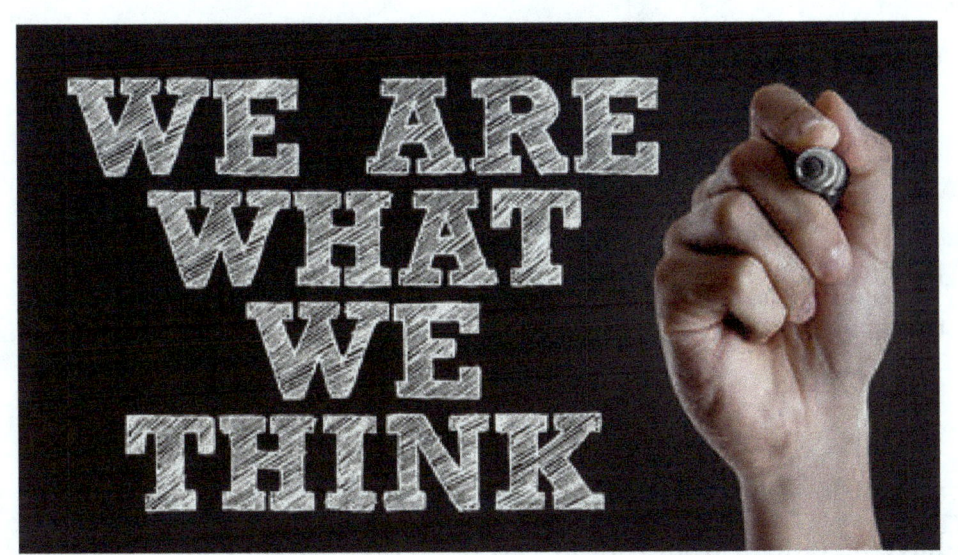

Chapter 10 Setting a Routine

When we were growing up, many of us used to be reminded the time to go to rest, and the time to wake up, when we need to do our homework, the time to shower, eat dinner and play with our friends.

However, this doesn't happen when we become adults. Many adults don't have a specific schedule for their day. In fact, most have no clue of what they are going to do once they wake up because they haven't decided to create a schedule to follow. Therefore, this makes many grown-ups to become stressed, overwhelmed, anxious and falling short of their true abilities.

The way to solve this is to create a routine timetable that works well for each one, and one that allows us to become productive, controlled, and the best person we can be.

I once saw a daily routine as monotonous and restrictive, which I'm sure is an opinion many shares. They live their life, thinking they are free somehow, in a wild and fantastic way. Rather, it has come to my attention that the way to liberty, productivity, joy is so we can realize our real potential is to develop and adhere to a routine. Hence, with a certain routine, we would all be better off.

If we follow a routine every day, the need to make choices every day is lessened. It allows us to understand precisely what duties we have to perform daily without too much contemplation. We understand what happens next without too much thought when we're done with one assignment. Activities are listed, which leads to greater efficiency.

When we design a routine thoroughly, our activities must be scheduled every morning, and our precious time must be allocated.

A daily routine offers our life framework and reasoning. It offers the basis for our life and events every day. We soon become acquainted with what we need to do daily and become comfortable. It allows us to experience the flow of current.

We spend free time on planning, decision-making, and training by following a routine. Our timetable has been predefined and enables us to use our time effectively. Repetitiveness is the key to healthy practices. It promotes the development of healthy behaviors, motivating us to do the same tasks whenever designing a private routine that works for us. Just as every morning, we adhere to a routine that enables us to promote practices which correspond to our objectives and ambitions.

While our routine enables us to build good practices to make full use of our potential, also, it makes us eliminate bad habits that don't work well for us. By repetition, we can slowly substitute our poor habits with excellent ones. This enables us to first and foremost achieve our goals when we design and follow through on our tasks. We understand the importance of completing our tasks, and the sense of accomplishment when we get to cross something off the list is quite rewarding.

The value of developing a certain routine obliges us to prioritize and to decide what we care about. We already understand what to do and what to do rather than take these choices every day, because we have scheduled them closely. After searching for my soul and looking closely at it, for instance, I decided to make sure I was conscientious and healthy so that I incorporated meditation and training into my routine.

Whenever a collection of tasks and activities become a routine, it cuts down the odds that we will postpone doing them. It becomes part of us to the point where we can do it subconsciously.

Repetition builds momentum, making it easier to continue when you do the same stuff repeatedly. This is why it's simpler to go to the gym; the more often you do it. The passage of time is an important factor in ensuring achievement and helping to create that momentum following a routine.

It enables to create trust and provides us with a feeling of enormous fulfillment when we adhere to and follow a routine. That gives us the fuel to carry on and take advantage of our routine. And one of the primary reasons why it is hard for individuals to alter their life for better is lack of self-confidence.

It can assist us in saving cash if we follow a routine and do the same stuff again and again. For example, every morning, juicing of fruit and vegetables is part of my routine. I can buy my fruits and vegetable in huge quantities, saving me cash because I understand that I'm going to follow this routine religiously. The same goes for much more, such as the price of membership in the long-term gym.

Certain things will always be beyond our control in our lives, and we must acknowledge that. However, we can regulate so much, particularly if we follow a routine. It cuts down on the pressure when we design and stick to a routine because we do not need to figure out what needs to happen next.

Rarely if ever, are our objectives and ambitions accomplished at once. Successful individuals achieve their objectives by repeatedly doing the same stuff. A sportsman gets excellent at his game if he continues to practice daily. An artist constantly repeats his craft.

One of the safest ways of ensuring your achievement is to develop and stick with a routine consistent with your objectives.

It's an excellent method to monitor progress. We can then create changes and return to our private routines while trusting that we're back on the correct track.

Be aware that it's all right if you decide to pursue your routine on weekends alone, or in case you have a different routine on Monday, Wednesday, and Friday. It's also completely all right to elect to do nothing. You have closely considered this and are aware of your decisions.

The main thing here is that you need to consider it and remain aware of your decisions exhaustively. A routine is a deliberate decision to live your life in a certain way. It is one of the secrets to success and good fortune. Each of us has specific wishes, needs, objectives, and resources.

Therefore, after thoroughly choosing what we want to accomplish in our life, it is essential that we create our own routines. It certainly is worth the attempt to reap the benefits. Today is a new day, and it is never too late to begin your routine.

"We are what we repeatedly do. Excellence, then, is not an act, but a habit."- Aristotle

Because I didn't want to live my life according to the regulations other people set for me, I struggled against developing healthy practices and routines. Besides, keeping a routine was hard work.

It turns out that it's much more emotionally exhausting to have no routine or structure whatsoever.

By avoiding to do what I knew would help me. For example, meditating, creating a list of gratitude and exercising, I took away the energy that these kinds of beneficial operations produce from my body and mind. Indoors and out, I felt tired. My dreams and objectives just fell away, leading to isolation and a feeling of helplessness.

Now, I am more motivated and passionate, which makes it possible for me to fulfill my goals. I have enough mental and bodily electricity to make my days interesting, even days when it is tough for me. I find happiness and more comfort with the excellent and depth of my life.

One of the changes I had to make for this to happen was to shift my view about routines. When I'm suffering through a depressive episode, I tend to rely heavily on making a schedule and sticking to it.

I admit it though: creating productive habits isn't effortless.

Here is something that you need to recall: what works for someone else doesn't mean that it will work for you. That is why it is important to choose tasks that go well with you. Go for tasks that allow you to become the better version of yourself, and maintain those tasks.

Don't be scared to keep your feet in fresh water and learn how it works for you. If they leave you feeling rejuvenated, then you need to hold to them. If they don't continue trying new ones until you find the right one, the secret is to build normal and steady patterns daily, that will push you to where you want in life, allowing you to take advantage of every stage as possible.

A daily hobby makes you attain laser-like attention from the time you rise in the morning to the time you close your eyes. Below are some ways to consider.

Be positive: Start the day with motivation. It could be anything, from positive affirmations to repeating one task you're determined to do that day. This kicks off your day with the right kind of mindset. Don't overwhelm yourself with a list of tasks right as you wake up; center on yourself first.

The purpose of this is to send a command from your conscious thinking to your subconscious mind. Your unconscious idea has to agree with what you say to it, and it will do anything to change the instructions into a reality.

Make sure your day-by-day to-do list is relatively short so that it is something that you can complete and not overwhelming.

An important technique to ensure that your list is easy is to apply the Post-It-Note. The measurements of a Post-It-Note are great because the size limit will make you to entirely record the most critical thing that you have to do every day.

Although each of the above tips is meant to help you move forward, sometimes, you only need to give yourself a break. Breaks will prevent you from getting bored and losing your concentration. At the same time, breaks will boost the function of your brain. It will force you to reevaluate what you are working on, making sure that you are moving in the right direction.

Subdividing your day into smaller tasks ensures that you remain at the top of your game.

While all of these tips are supposed to help you forge ahead, on occasion you just need to step again and give your thinking a break.

If you spend a lot of time doing just one thing, it can make you lose your interest and focus. And if you are working on a task you hate doing; it makes it less difficult because you will only be doing a little of it.

Spend your time working on what you want by optimizing the output in the least time. The way you value your time and use it is what is important. Try to review your day and figure out how you can divide it up into blocks of time, where you also have time for recreation.

It is fine to become flexible when it comes to building new habits. In other words, be specific on what you are searching for, but maintain the flexibility to work inside your lifestyle so your habits can stick.

No two days are ever the same. Our mental energy might be prepared to complete tasks one day and totally depleted the next.

So, if you can't do it all at once, that's okay. Don't feel guilty or like you're not productive enough. The American Psychological Association suggests that to enhance our success, we should focus on one goal at a time.

Chapter 11 Exercises to apply to daily life

You can't always rely on your unconscious habits (whether good or bad) to do all the work for you. Sometimes, you have to make deliberate thoughts, decisions, and actions to help move you forward in life. Until now, it is likely that many of the actions you have taken in your life are backed by pesky little habits like negative self-talk, poor self-confidence, or your commitment to staying comfortable. However, not every single action you make is a habit and so, when you arrive at new decisions, you need to know how to consciously take action in your life and move forward intentionally and successfully in the right direction. In this chapter, I'm going to show you how I was able to stop making weak decisions at every turn and start taking bold, confident and focused action in my life.

Awakening is a state of calm awareness. In a state of awakening, you are in a heightened awareness of your body. It can be incredibly soothing and relaxing and can work wonders when you are attempting to control your own behaviors. Learning these exercises could work wonders for your self-regulation skills, and will allow you to better regulate yourself. When you are feeling stressed, tense, overwhelmed, or any other negative feelings, reverting to some of these methods could help you immensely to maintain control over yourself and find some calm relaxation.

Stillness

Though it may seem sort of counterintuitive, stillness, freezing up, can provide you with a sort of awakening of its own without requiring anything but your body and a quiet space to stop. Do not think about anything at this moment. Take a deep breath and clear your mind.

Do not focus on your breathing or your body, simply the stillness that is surrounding you. Focus on the quiet, inviting stillness and find comfort there.

As you are there, allow yourself to be at peace. Accept yourself for who you are, for what you do, and for how you behave. There is no criticism during this time—only calm acceptance and you should be able to find solace in that. Make sure you continue to breathe, slowly, rhythmically, and methodically. With every breath in, allow your tension, your worry, and your fears to gather within you. With every breath out, let it go. Release those feelings into the world and no longer worry about them. Let yourself set yourself free and enjoy it.

Your body will slowly begin to relax. You will enter a state of calmness. Allow yourself to remain in that state, healing, loving yourself, and accepting yourself for who you are. Then let the breath go.

Restore Your Attention

This method of awakening involves collecting your thoughts. It allows you to focus your attention on the world around you, gathering that attention and being able to remain vigilant and mindful as you walk through the world. You should be able to feel your wellbeing improve as you do this, recognizing that you are becoming more confident and determined in yourself as you go through the process. You can use this quietly any time you are feeling overwhelmed or as if you cannot function or focus any longer.

Choose an area to take a walk. It could be through your neighborhood, at a park, on a nature trail, or anything else. As you begin your walk, focus on each and every individual thing you see. Focus on the forms you see and count them. Any structure can be a form. As you walk, label whatever it is and count it while you walk. If you see a bird, note that and count one.

As you keep going, you see a tree, count two. Another step, you see a dandelion, that's three. You keep going, looking at everything around you and counting as you go. Eventually, you will stop thinking as you do so. You will eventually enter a quiet, calm state in which all that exists in the world around you as a whole, rather than individual objects, and you will find your mind peacefully quiet.

Awareness of Your Breathing

Breathing is essential to your very being. You need it to survive. Without it, you will die. You can trigger a state of awakening through awareness of your breathing if you sit back, relax, and let the breathing come naturally.

When you are attempting this, start sitting down. You should cross your legs, rest your hands on your legs, and straighten yourself into a proper posture. Do not hold onto excess tension—it will only distract you from the proper goal. When you are sitting there, relaxed and comfortable, you are ready to start breathing. There are several different breathing techniques you can use for triggering your state of calmness that you can find all over the internet and in other books as well. For now, this book will offer you two different breathing techniques:

The One Minute Breath

This type of breathing is believed to help clear your mind and soothe any anxiety or fear you may be feeling in the moment. It is quite simple, though it may take some practice to learn to execute properly. The end goal is to spread your breath to an entire minute for a single breath. You would inhale for 20 seconds, slowly filling your lungs with air. You would hold the air for 20 seconds, allowing it to rest in your lung and remain there. Lastly, you would exhale your breath for 20 seconds before starting again. This process should be repeated for at least three minutes for an ideal effect.

If this seems too daunting or your lungs are not strong enough yet, you can start with 5-second intervals, in which you draw your breath for 5 seconds, hold for 5 seconds, and exhale for 5 seconds and slowly push yourself until you can take one breath in a minute. Again, ensure you are repeating the process for at least 3 minutes at a time.

The Cooling Breath

This breath has you inhale through your mouth, across your tongue. Your tongue should be twisted into a U shape, with the tip of the rolled tongue sticking just past the lips. You should leave it there and inhale through your tongue like a straw, sucking the air and letting it fill your lungs. The air will be cold. Hold the breath in your lungs for a few seconds, then exhale through your nose. Make sure you are doing this for at least three minutes for best results. This type of breathing is meant to calm your nervous system, soothing nerves, and helping you relax.

Mindful Meditation

This exercise will help you draw yourself inwards, relaxing and soothing yourself as you allow your mind to rest.

Start by sitting. Find somewhere comfortable and quiet and settle yourself down, resting quietly. Cross your legs in front of you and straighten your spine without stiffening up. Allow your arms to rest naturally, with your hands resting on your legs. Let your chin drop slightly; your eyes will naturally drift downward and that is okay. Sit in this position for a few moments, focusing on your breathing. Feel the air travel through your lungs and your body before exhaling. Focus on the feeling of the air coming in and out with your breaths. If your mind wanders, that is okay. Observe whatever it is your mind is focusing on, quietly and without judgment, and calmly redirect back. It is okay to get distracted sometimes, and you might learn something about yourself when you follow a thought that is catching your attention.

After a predetermined amount of time, or whenever you are ready, open your eyes or lift your gaze up. Listen to the world around you, calmly. Pay attention to how you are feeling at that moment. What are you thinking about? What are you feeling? Take a moment to simply revel in the feeling, enjoying the quiet moment, and then move on with your day.

Yoga

The entire purpose of yoga is to reach a state of mindful awakening through rhythmic, calming movements and stretches. You exercise while relaxing your body, slowly strengthening, stretching, and feeling each muscle relax. Your mind calms as you breathe steadily. You feel calm and at ease. There are several poses for a wide range of different purposes and skill levels. This section will introduce a basic calming pose.

Child's Pose

The child's pose is a beginner's pose that can be used for resting, clearing of the mind, and reducing stress while stretching out the legs, hips, and back.

Start by getting down on your hands and knees. Take a deep breath and encourage your mind to clear. Focus on how the breath feels in your lungs. Spread your knees while keeping your feet and toes touching. Relax backward, allowing your buttocks to fall and rest on the heels of your feet. Modify this however necessary to get a general position—pregnant women should modify this pose to avoid pressure on their bellies. If you have tight hips, you can keep your legs together instead of stretching them out.

Sit up and stretch your spine, feeling it straighten between your head and your tailbone. Take in another deep breath, and as you exhale, allow your torso and arms to slide forward. Your chest should be between your thighs and your forehead to the floor, with your arms stretched outward and your palms against the floor. Relax your back, allowing tension to melt away from your torso. Hold your pose and breathe deeply and softly. As you release the pose, slowly push yourself upward with your hands and sit back on your heels.

Awareness of Posture

Your posture can control the way you feel. If you are hunched over, hiding within yourself and trying to make yourself as small as you possibly can, you are not going to feel calm or soothed. You can alter the way you feel through being aware of how you are standing, and if you are mindful about the ways that you are able to stand and how you feel when you stand in certain poses and postures, you will be able to relax. You may even find awakening in doing so, a heightened sense of awareness of what is happening within your body.

Start by acknowledging how you are standing. Release the tension that is clinging to your body. Shake out your shoulders or your back and allow the tension to melt away. You should stand straight up, with your spine straight and aligned, and allow yourself to relax. Stretch your spine, allowing the tension to travel through your spine and through your legs, into the ground.

Loosen your shoulders and hold your head high, but relaxed. You do not want to trigger aggression or anger, but rather a sense of quiet calmness in which you can retreat and reflect.

You can do this sitting down as well, legs crossed and with your hands resting gently on your legs. You should be able to feel the tension melt away with your deep breaths. Quiet your mind and listen to your breathing, counting them as they come in and out slowly but surely.

Self-Massage

Start with your hands on your knees. Straighten out your back and neck and make sure you are stretched out and comfortable. Take in a deep breath and allow your shoulders to move forward. They should move forward, and then up, moving toward your eyes and ears. As you exhale, allow your shoulders to finish rolling around and then back down into their natural position. Take another deep breath as you let your shoulders relax. Take in another deep breath and repeat this process for another minute.

After the minute has passed and your shoulders are relaxed into their natural positions again, take a deep breath and exhale. One more deep breath and push your shoulders back up, stretching them as far as you can and holding them there for a moment. After a few seconds have passed and you are ready to exhale, do so as you let your shoulders fall back to their natural spot.

This allows you to release the tension you may be holding in your neck and shoulders, and doing so can allow you to relax further. The breathing can help you work toward a state of awakening as the warm sensation of having stretched and relaxed your shoulders and neck spreads and circulates.

Conclusion

I hope you become unbiased, strong, pure, positive and free from all fears. By gaining knowledge on all topics mentioned you will learn how to tackle your mind to balance it between stress and happiness. Don't lodge subconscious mind with any negativity.

Practice all the exercises and good habits to maintain your physical and mental health. After reading this book you should have complete control on your thoughts and desire for filling it with all the positive assertions. Make your personality strong that no evil can contaminate you. Keep laughing every day and spread love and joy to all your loved ones. Be stable and calm so that you don't linger between the extremes. Fill your heart with joy and not with grief of sorrow and misery. Always be close to God, he is the controller of our life. Do good deeds because sooner or later the day will come when we have to answer him about our actions.

I hope that my readers enjoyed this book. I wish you always remember all the tips I suggested for being happy and positive throughout your life. Recall all the positive affirmations regularly and practice all the exercises every day to maintain good health.

www.ingramcontent.com/pod-product-compliance
Lightning Source LLC
Chambersburg PA
CBHW051705160426

43209CB00004B/1032